What's Stopping You?

Why Smart People Don't Always Reach Their Potential, and How You Can

2nd edition

Robert Kelsey

CAPSTONE

This updated second edition first published 2012
© 2012 What's Stopping You Ltd
What's Stopping You? is a trademark of What's Stopping You Ltd

First edition published 2011

Registered office
Capstone Publishing Ltd (A Wiley Company), John Wiley and Sons Ltd, The Atrium, Southern Gate, Chichester, West Sussex, PO19 8SQ, United Kingdom

For details of our global editorial offices, for customer services and for information about how to apply for permission to reuse the copyright material in this book please see our website at www.wiley.com.

Wiley publishes in a variety of print and electronic formats and by print-on-demand. Some material included with standard print versions of this book may not be included in e-books or in print-on-demand. If this book refers to media such as a CD or DVD that is not included in the version you purchased, you may download this material at http://booksupport.wiley.com. For more information about Wiley products, visit www.wiley.com.

Designations used by companies to distinguish their products are often claimed as trademarks. All brand names and product names used in this book are trade names, service marks, trademarks or registered trademarks of their respective owners. The publisher is not associated with any product or vendor mentioned in this book. This publication is designed to provide accurate and authoritative information in regard to the subject matter covered. It is sold on the understanding that the publisher is not engaged in rendering professional services. If professional advice or other expert assistance is required, the services of a competent professional should be sought.

While the case studies outlined in the pages ahead are based on concerns and experiences outlined to the author – either directly or indirectly – all names and locations have been changed in order to protect identities. Also, in all the case studies sufficient details and circumstances have been altered for any resemblance to real persons, living or dead, to be purely coincidental.

Library of Congress Cataloging-in-Publication Data

Kelsey, Robert, 1964-
  What's stopping you? : why smart people don't always reach their potential, and how you can / Robert Kelsey. – 2nd ed.
      p. cm.
  Includes index.
  ISBN 978-0-85708-307-4 (pbk.)
  1. Success in business. 2. Self-actualization (Psychology) 3. Self-help techniques. I. Title.
  HF5386.K275 2012
  650.1–dc23

                                                                2012016640

A catalogue record for this book is available from the British Library.

ISBN 978-0-857-08307-4 (paperback) ISBN 978-0-857-08336-4 (ebk)
ISBN 978-0-857-08337-1 (ebk) ISBN 978-0-857-08338-8 (ebk)

Set in 10/13.5 pt Sabon by Toppan Best-set Premedia Limited
Printed in Great Britain by International Ltd, Padstow, Cornwall, UK

CONTENTS

To Lucy

PREFACE TO THE SECOND EDITION

I had high hopes for *What's Stopping You?* when it was first published in April 2011. But I also nursed many doubts. As a High-FF (all explained within), this was perhaps inevitable. Fear of failure makes our doubts cast long shadows over our hopes and, before long, we are sabotaging ourselves with our negative self-beliefs.

For those with a high fear of failure this is a well known cycle. And one that, usually, results in arrested endeavour – potentially followed by frustration, depression, anger and resignation. Well not this time. Encouraged by my agent (Isabel Atherton at Creative Authors), my publisher (Holly Bennion at Wiley) and my wife (Lucy), I took the plunge. I wrote about the fears and doubts and insecurities that have plagued me since childhood, and about the research I've undertaken over many years to try and fathom out my condition.

What's Stopping You? is the result and, so far, its reception has bowled me over. Originally published in April 2011, the book reached Number One in a major retail business book chart around May and stayed there until January 2012. It also won positive reviews, professional praise and, literally, hundreds of emails from readers that felt the book spoke to them personally and was helping them understand their condition and plot a more productive path.

Fear of failure is a mass condition, although one that often goes unrecognized in sufferers. And, after reading the book, many of those writing to me expressed the feeling that they now felt equipped for the (far from easy) journey ahead. They better understood the fears and doubts that prevented them making progress in their careers and personal pursuits and were more willing to accept who they were, including their own faulty wiring. And this realization was helping them chart a more sustainable, as well as positive, path ahead. It was also helping them deal with the inevitable barriers along the way.

As stated within, praise is a valuable currency for those with fear of failure, so my heartfelt thanks to those that offered it.

The book's warm reception and strong sales has led to this second edition. In some cases the new edition tackles the "constructive criticism" offered by readers (usually a contradiction in terms for the High-FF). Though mainly it includes additional content based on reader requests. Primarily, this means the inclusion of 19 case studies. Mostly, these are people who contacted me following publication, although I do occasionally take a punt on a well-known or historical name, highlighting behaviour that is useful for illustrating the book's needs.

Another addition to this edition is the *Seven Steps to Navigating Fear of Failure*. To be honest, I shied away from adding exercises in the original book. In my view, too many self-help books lapse into pointless and even nonsensical exercises, almost as an alternative to constructive prose aimed at understanding our frailties. "Say 'I am loved and I am loveable' in the mirror 25 times each morning" – that sort of thing (an actual exercise in one of my source books, I kid you not) – will soon have the reader feeling confused and mildly humiliated, which is exactly the sort of emotion High-FFs spend their lives avoiding. And, anyway, I was writing primarily for a British market (by which I mean for the Brits' natural reserve more than our geographical location) that may find such emotionally charged and self-regarding activities, frankly, silly.

That said, the book's stated aim is to help readers draw their own map of the future – something authentically theirs as they forge their own path through the jungle. This, indeed, involves "exercises" such as calculating our *true values* and visualizing ourselves in 10 years' time. So I've added a final section that summarizes these needs. This means that the narrative of the book remains – allowing the reader to absorb the text in the knowledge that any required proactivity on their part will be handily reiterated at the end.

There are also some amendments to the narrative itself – mostly based on reader feedback. For instance, entrepreneurship is far from the only *Me Inc.* route, so there are added sections on freelancing and franchising or simply on adopting a new attitude within your current employment. And I have been more exploratory regarding High-FF traits – especially my own – many of which (such as rebelliousness in childhood) are far from obvious.

So please keep the feedback coming (via my website at www. robert-kelsey.co.uk). Or perhaps attend one of my "fear of failure" events. But most of all please keep pursuing an *understanding* of who you are, which should be part of a process towards *accepting* yourself – including your insecurities – and *navigating* your way towards a better future.

Robert Kelsey, recovering High-FF

FOREWORD BY LUKE JOHNSON

Most of us know that the secret to success is confidence. Good looks, intelligence, qualifications – all these help, but with many of the highest achievers I've met, their greatest asset has been their world class chutzpah.

Unfortunately, many of us don't possess such bountiful self-assurance. We are racked with doubts. We focus too much on the losing shots, not our aces. So Robert Kelsey has written a book for the rest of us, everyone who lacks confidence, who can be too self-critical, who isn't sure if they're up to it or going to make it. And I think it's a winner.

The truth is that such feelings are self-fulfilling. Just as the confident person creates the mental conditions for their own success, the person who lacks confidence creates the mental conditions for their lack of progress. This makes fear of failure a debilitating condition but also one where improvement is possible, not least because failure is the very thing that confident people don't fear. As Robert Kelsey proves, the ability to fall flat on your face without it undermining your desire to keep trying is perhaps the most important quality those high-chutzpah types possess.

Certainly, success is not about being ambitious – that's easy. It's about overcoming adversity. And in my experience, what separates the winners and the losers in life is how they handle disappointment. Achievement in any field is impossible without setbacks.

What separates the field is not the setback, however, but the response to it.

This book offers help to those that, up until now, have been stymied by setbacks – indeed, may have even avoided participation for fear of encountering a setback. Yet the great point of the author's advice is that it is both philosophical with regard to the nature of fear and its impact on achievement, and practical. For those who may be paralyzed by a fear of failure, it offers a way through – not through the impractical nonsense of many self-help books, but through step-by-step advice on the fears that attack us at each stage, and how we can think and act differently for a better outcome. The remarkable sales of the first edition of this book are proof that Robert's message has resonated with thousands of readers.

The author has not invented a new philosophy or programme for living. Rather he has summarized the contents of scores of relevant self-help books – picking the bits that work, ignoring the elements that don't. His aim is to create a tailored route for those who may simply be trying to avoid failure – helping them get a better result. There are, after all, reams of such volumes in print. And while some are useful, many of them are not. The author has covered the waterfront, and has selected the most useful and reliable advice from his research of hundreds of psychologists, therapists and self-help gurus.

What's Stopping You? is also a highly personal book. The author talks in depth about his career journey, how he overcame his own demons by studying the literature, by really analyzing his own issues, and by developing techniques to deal with them. Sometimes amusing, sometimes cringing, sometimes painful – his own experiences add to the impression that this is a book written from the heart, even if it is aimed squarely at the head.

Robert Kelsey is a rare beast because he runs his own business – but he can also actually write. He participates and he also reports – and thinks deeply about the challenges. Word processing has enabled everyone to churn out reams of material. But few who tackle these types of subjects actually have any literary ability: in reality their prose style can be awful. Poor writing makes a book hard to read and difficult to remember – and more than anything I enjoyed reading this book. And that makes a difference when so many business and self-help books are bought and never read – partly because they are essentially unreadable. But Mr Kelsey's text is highly enjoyable and eminently fluent.

Not all the tips here will work for everyone. But there is a sufficient range of topics for any reader – and especially any reader that has suffered from a debilitating lack of confidence – to find something relevant to their situation: from goal setting to handling work colleagues, from discovering your true values and motivations to starting a business.

So I wholeheartedly endorse this book, and encourage the casual reader to put it on their bedside table and browse it at regular intervals: for inspiration, for understanding, and for pragmatic advice. I've enjoyed reading it, and I think you will too.

Luke Johnson
Chairman of Risk Capital Partners and
the Royal Society for the Encouragement of Arts,
Manufacturers and Commerce

INTRODUCTION

"Failure is not an option," said the actor playing Gene Kranz, flight director for Mission Control in *Apollo 13*, the 1995 movie dramatizing the near-disaster of the third Apollo mission to the Moon. But he was wrong. It *was* an option, which is why he said it. Kranz knew that his team had to think the unthinkable, invent the uninvented, do the undoable. And this meant employing classic alpha-male posturing to force them beyond their *fear of failure*.

He knew that failure was staring them in the face but, given the consequences of failure, any other option was not only preferable but imperative. Had he said "failure is almost certain, but let's have a go anyway" his team would have been unable to get beyond their fear of public humiliation for suggesting a potentially daft idea. Yet daft ideas were the only thing that could save the astronauts, so Kranz had to find a way of getting them on the table – hence upping the stakes in order to overcome his team's individual fears.

Fear of failure

Yet *Apollo 13* is a movie and those words were written by a script-writer (despite the real Gene Kranz later adopting them for the title of his biography). The fears that prevent us from achieving our goals are usually private, mundane, nuanced and sometimes so subtle that many of us may not fully accept their impact on our thoughts and actions.

As Kranz knew, fear of failure can change our behaviour in ways that render failure a near certainty. Fear paralyzes our decision-making, throws our judgment, destroys our creativity and removes previously easy fluidity from even everyday movements. Yet as mental conditions go, fear of failure is not only one of the most common – with millions of sufferers in the UK alone – it is also one of the least acknowledged or acted upon, partly because those with the condition are so paralyzed by their fear of humiliation or public embarrassment they suffer in silence, or even in self-denial, rather than seek treatment.

They are chained to the seabed, unable to swim towards the sunlight above due to their fears and insecurities. Of course, some may express their fears through depression or anger without even realizing what lies behind such symptoms – making them hostage to behaviour that further confirms their inner fears and further destroys their potential for progress.

And while the actor playing Kranz unlocked the potential of his team with one powerful phrase, we are unlikely to be so lucky. Even if we acknowledge our fears and seek to overcome them, we may find ourselves bewildered by the hundreds of self-help books offering more confidence, higher self-esteem, greater success and even "unlimited power." Some deal directly with fear of failure. Others focus on related or underlying conditions such as lack of confidence or low self-esteem. Many offer a near-instant cure – the banishment of our frailties and the certainty of success – through a mental realignment injected into us via some, admittedly strong, motivational words and techniques.

But a health warning is required. Promising the chance to be born again as a new, more-confident, even fearless person is a false promise made to afflicted people desperate for a cure. Conditions such as fear of failure – as well as antecedents such as low self-esteem – are, as we shall see, innate. Once and however inflicted they are here to stay.

That's the bad news. The good news is that we can understand our insecurities, accept them as part of us and make strong progress while taking them into account. In fact, in my opinion strong sustainable progress is *only* possible once we have accepted that our fears and primary beliefs are here to stay. We can develop a strong self-awareness of our fear-driven behaviours – and their root causes – and we can learn to live with who we are. We don't have to banish our fears forever in order to move forward. Indeed, we can achieve our goals. As long as they are the right goals, *our* goals – not false goals potentially fed to us by external influences or our own faulty thinking.

And that's where this book comes in. People with a fear of failure need a map. This book is not a map. In fact, we have to draw our own map and even that will require many redrafts before being even vaguely accurate. What this book provides, I hope, is guidance on how to go about drawing such a map: in draft, fuzzy at the edges, containing plenty of "here be dragons" elements, but a map nonetheless. Something we can grasp and regard as we cut through the thicket. Something that allows us to take those all-important next steps.

The monkey on my back

I have suffered from a debilitating fear of failure all my life – itself the result of poor confidence brought about by a low self-esteem developed in early childhood. At key moments in my life fear has led me to doubt my abilities to succeed, which has profoundly changed my behaviour in ways that made success less likely: often snatching a humiliating defeat from the jaws of victory. And I have read scores of books in an effort to shift what I call the "monkey on my back" – the creature that whispers fear and self-doubt in my ear at critical moments.

But the monkey hasn't disappeared. In fact, there was no shifting him, which didn't seem to compute with the literature I was reading, much of which promised both a cure for my insecurities and the certainty of dream fulfilment. Clearly, I was doing something wrong: perhaps not applying the methodology diligently enough or maintaining destructive behaviours and beliefs. Yet I now realize it was their prognosis that was flawed because it took too little account of the fact I am who I am, and that the monkey comes too.

Surely a more powerful book would describe a route towards progress from our own flawed perspective – answering the question "what's stopping you?" with the answer: you are (and the monkey of course). Yet it would also state that we must accept the monkey as a fellow passenger and plan to make progress anyway. It would spot and describe the likely barriers preventing progress, as well as the false assumptions they may generate.

Certainly, if we could see that it was our responses to those barriers that were producing the poor results, not the barriers themselves – nor was it poor luck, innate ineptitude or even prejudice against us – then we may be able to generate better results.

We don't need a miracle cure injected into us. We just need to take account of our insecurities and navigate our way forward accordingly.

A practitioner in failure

I am a practitioner in failure with a childhood and early adulthood punctuated with one self-fulfilling educational and career disaster after another.

Written-off as stupid by low-grade village-school teachers, and traumatized by the immediately preceding break-up of my family, I failed the 11-plus and ended up in an Essex secondary-modern turned comprehensive school. I left aged 15 with just one O level. Directionless, I was taken on by a local building surveyor needing someone to hold a stripy pole in muddy fields, although he kindly enrolled me on a day-a-week diploma course. Inevitably, I bunked the course – instead spending the days walking the streets of London with a day-return ticket in my pocket.

This eventually landed me a job looking after the vast residential property portfolio of the London region's gas board. I was 18 at the time and loved it. I was working for a large West End surveying firm full of graduates and professionals, who were nice to me despite my gruff accent and manners. They encouraged me to return to education, so – realizing I was as capable as them – I enrolled on an evening A level history course and, five years later, graduated from the University of Manchester with a high 2:1 joint-honours degrees in Politics & Modern History.

But I was, again, directionless, other than a vague notion of going into journalism – a highly competitive trade rarely conquered through the application of vague notions. Yet after a few false turns I managed to land a staff-writer then editor's role for a banking-focused magazine, which ultimately resulted in me becoming a banker in what the City describes as a "gamekeeper turned poacher move."

As I relay in Part One, I was not a great banker. Paralyzed by fear, I worked in both London and the US before realizing I was simply not cut out for finance. Once again without a plan, I was recruited by a friend with a plan – for a dotcom "incubator" (this was the height of the dotcom boom) – and together we founded *Metrocube*, an "e-business community" that incubated over 200 companies before being sold a few years after the dotcom crash.

Cured of my journalistic and banking ambitions, and somewhat bitten by the entrepreneurial bug, I then combined my skills and experiences to start *Moorgate Communications*, a financial public relations agency aimed at banks, which has been a sustainable and fulfilling enterprise ever since – even growing through the financial meltdown of 2008–09.

Oh, and I wrote a book on my banking experiences in New York, which was published in 2000 and had me all set – I thought – for a career as a humorous, laddish writer in the Nick Hornby or Michael Lewis mould. However, the book sold less than I'd hoped and my dream was dashed.

An addiction to self-help

The book-writing career aside, it is possible to read the above and think I am, in fact, a long way from a practitioner in failure. But that's because I have edited out the fears, frustrations, moods, paranoia, anguish and temper tantrums that have punctuated every one of the above experiences. Terrorized by my own insecurities, I have been a nightmare to work with and apologize now to any colleagues that had to suffer my nonsense.

But I have also made considerable progress in facing up to my fears and insecurities. Perhaps surprisingly given my earlier comments, much of this has been due to my ongoing addiction to self-help books. This began while in the US – where the acres of shelves dedicated to the genre suggest an openness that the UK is only slowly adopting – although it took a deeper hold of me back in the UK as I began to realize the problem was not a particular job or person or set of circumstances. The problem was me.

Ultimately, and as described within, this landed me in the hands of a professional psychotherapist. Yet far from complementing the work of all those self-help gurus, the therapist – plus further research of my own – opened my eyes to the gaping hole between what the psychologists state about our innate (but treatable) personalities and the near-instant and life-changing promises and cures on offer from the self-help gurus.

My first reaction to this was – not untypically – anger. The gurus seemed to be offering false hope and unrealistic dreams that could ultimately leave people further weakened. But then the penny dropped. Much of what they convey has been incredibly useful. Their tips and techniques can be both logical and inspiring. Someone rejecting their divinity with respect to the earthly paradise promised can, therefore, still make use of their, often very practical, advice and methodologies – many of which pepper the pages ahead.

Certainly I still fight the fear every day, as well as my low self-esteem. But I now realize this is part of my chemistry and that such a chemistry doesn't condemn me. It just means I must take it into account. And it is both the flawed thinking and behaviour of those with a high fear of failure – as well as related insecurities such as low self-esteem – and the progress possible despite it, that I wish to convey in this book.

> **What's Stopping You?** *Your insecurities are part of your chemistry. They cannot be removed through instant cures. Yet strong progress is possible once you realize who you are and take this into account.*

PART ONE

What *is* Stopping You?

1

FEAR

Ask what was stopping *me* and I can tell you immediately: fear. Fear of failure in fact. Relationship-issues with parents, siblings, teachers and peers can be a cause, as can other traumatic events in childhood – especially ones where we feel demeaned or humiliated. But the fear can build from tiny beginnings into an uncontrollable phobia that can mentally paralyze the sufferer in adulthood. It can also strike us at various stages in our career – even once we have built up strong confidence in a particular area.

My disastrous investment banking "career" provides a potent example in my own story. A seemingly confident financial journalist with a strong and detailed knowledge of corporate banking, I caught the eye of a leading corporate bank and, after a protracted interview and assessment process, persuaded them I had the perfect training and background for joining their growing corporate banking team within the investment bank.

Yet once inside the door my behaviour changed. I became fearful that my knowledge was paper-thin and I possessed nothing more than a talent for empty bravado. Of course, this was probably true, but was no different to the majority of bankers in the room – all with very narrow experience compared to my breadth of knowledge across the corporate banking spectrum (exactly the knowledge required for selling the corporate bank's range of financial products). But having sold myself well during the recruitment process, once a practicing banker I became scared of putting a foot wrong

– leaving them wondering what had happened to the confident, even cocky, person they'd employed as their next hotshot "originator."

My role was to source US$100 million-plus financings for the bank to arrange and distribute to investors. As a journalist, these deals looked easy. I assumed the bank found a willing borrower, asked for some security (in this case trade-receivables such as oil shipments), handed over the money and waited for it to come back with interest. But half the banks in London were doing the same, forcing me into one of the scariest margins of the 1990s corporate borrower universe: Russia.

In the mid-1990s businessmen were being gunned down on a daily basis on the streets of Moscow, and my clients – the newly privatized Russian oil companies – were certainly menacing organizations to deal with. Yet that wasn't the bit that scared me. In fact that helped mask my real terror, which was the bank discovering how little I knew about how to structure one of these deals. I couldn't calculate the volumes of oil required to repay the loan, or establish what volumes had to be where, when, and how they got there. It looked way too complex for my simple brain.

And the fact no one in the bank had this knowledge – we simply took the information on trust from the oil companies – didn't seem to bother anyone but me, which was a key part of my problem with banking. Taking such risks is the nuts and bolts of the industry. Yet I couldn't help visualizing one of about 20 disaster scenarios being played out in various hostile environments somewhere out there in the post-Soviet steppes – all of which would have rendered my banking career over in a puff of public humiliation.

Blind to office politics

Being risk-averse and technically inept should not have meant curtains for my banking career. Fear stalked the corridors of the entire bank – as did technical ineptitude come to that. The ultimate reason for failing as an investment banker was that all those technically inept and risk-averse bankers prospered by being hotshots at office politics. They had strong judgement regarding where the bank was heading and could make self-enhancing decisions on that basis.

But I was awful at office politics. And I had terrible judgement – based on trying to hide my fears and insecurities rather than focusing on the interests of the bank (or myself) – which led me to trust the wrong people and back the wrong deals. My behaviour changed to the point where I came across as a fool, and soon started being treated as one. Any deal on my desk looked dodgy for the simple reason it was on *my* desk, and any new project that came my way soon acquired a distinctly hot-potato feel to it.

Even the transfer to America – sold to me as the "move that could make you" – was no more than turning-out-the-lights on a failing office. The only way I could make it work was by discovering the one entity that would hoover up our loan structures no matter what: Enron.

Yet rather than focus on the skills required to become a competent banker – especially the soft skills such as calculating who could and couldn't be trusted and recruiting people to my cause – I soon sought a way out of banking. I fell back on my core skill of journalism and started writing about my life in New York, which before long had a greater hold on my imagination, and time, than a banking career that I was rejecting, seemingly before it could reject me.

Emotions and their role in survival

I detail the fears and behaviour that destroyed my banking career because they seem odd given that it took some guts to win the job in the first place. And I had clearly been judged as having the required knowledge and at least the capabilities of learning the trade by my seniors within the bank. Yet, as we shall see, those suffering from fear of failure are often able to take extreme risks in situations where failure is almost certain. Meanwhile, they find themselves paralyzed by everyday situations that involve only moderate but often very public risks. And they are more than capable of changing their behaviour in ways that make failure more likely. All of which makes fear of failure a debilitating and self-fulfilling condition seemingly at odds with today's career needs.

So how did we get to the point where so many people sabotage their own advancement through such self-harming behaviour? In his book *Emotion: the Science of Sentiment* (2001), British philosopher Dylan Evans tackles this conundrum by asking an important question: given the fact emotions such as fear and sadness seem to be "hardwired" into humans, why are they so bad for modern careers? Or looking at it the other way: as such emotions seem to offer no economic advantage – in fact just the opposite – why have they not died out in the process of natural selection?

He wonders why we have not evolved to behave like Spock in *Star Trek* and judge life's trials in purely logical terms. The conclusion appears to be that Spock's home planet of *Vulcan* was an abundant paradise entirely free of disease or predators. Meanwhile on Earth, Evans contests that emotions evolved as a rapid-reflexive action aimed at survival – hence it often arriving in an uncontrollable nerve-surge through the body.

Joy, distress, disgust, fear, anger: all played a key role in helping our survival in the "state of nature," says Evans. And to an extent we rarely acknowledge, such emotions continue to play an important evaluation role today, just a more subtle one. Evans provides evidence of this by observing those unable to use their emotions for evaluation.

"Those that lose their emotional capacity through brain damage tend to be easy victims for the unscrupulous," he observes. "Forced to rely on their logical reasoning, they make disastrous choices about whom they can trust."

Impaired mental capacity

Evans makes an important point because, as we shall see, those of us with fear of failure may well have such fears due to an impaired mental capacity when it comes to reasoning and evaluations – perhaps due to poor conditioning or traumatic events as a child. And this means that we are also vulnerable, with fear being our response to that vulnerability.

So emotions remain important in the modern world, which means that an impaired capacity to use our emotions to evaluate situations is potentially disastrous – or at best paralyzing.

Does this therefore enslave us to the potency of our emotions, forcing those with impaired evaluations into self-destructive behaviour? Not always. Plenty of people behave in ways not dictated by their emotions. The stiff upper-lip of the English upper classes is no myth, but is an external response rather than inward feeling – a training from an early age to hide emotions rather than change them – not dissimilar to the poker face of the professional gambler who may inwardly be in emotional turmoil. Yet such responses are only ever a mask. In reality "quiet desperation is the English way" – at least according to *Pink Floyd*.

Such masking takes training and is, in any case, an unsatisfactory response in the modern world where we are encouraged to express ourselves, or at least to behave in ways that generate trust and understanding rather than distrust and misunderstanding. And such a masking may simply delay a terrible reckoning – a breakdown as the mask slips and then collapses due to the pressure. Far better, surely, to try and understand our emotions, as well as how emotions such as fear can motivate and demotivate us, and how they can impair our evaluations and change our behaviours. Surely self-awareness trumps self-denial every time?

Experiments in emotional manipulation

In his book *Motivation* (1975) psychologist Phil Evans details the relatively short history of academic experiments on our emotions – and particularly on fear – and how they impact our motivation.

For instance, in 1948 the pioneering American psychologist Neal Miller experimented on the impact of fear on behaviour by placing rats in a box with two compartments – one black, one white – with those in the white zone consistently given electric shocks. The rats were soon exhibiting great reluctance to venture into the white zone, even overcoming physical barriers in order to escape to the safety of the black zone. And before long, Miller's harassed rodents needed only to catch sight of the white zone to exhibit signs of extreme stress. Miller concluded that fear as a driver can be quickly acquired, can change behaviour profoundly, and can internally condition the rat to elicit a fear response when subsequently triggered (i.e. when reminded of the trauma).

Unsurprisingly, such emotional conditioning is also applicable with humans, at even a subtle level. Evans cites Judson S. Brown a post-war American psychologist who thought that, due to fear, humans spend much of their time in search of "reinforcers" such as money and in performing "operant responses" such as holding down a job. In Brown's opinion, what a person was seeking was potentially less important than what a person was avoiding. He considered that a person could be said to be making money, but could equally be motivated by the fear of *not* making money.

For me, Brown's focus on avoidance is beginning to get to the heart of the matter with respect to fear as a driver. Yet when studying fear's motivational potential the most important contribution comes from John W. Atkinson of Stanford University.

In the 1960s Atkinson undertook a series of experiments on children that was to nail fear of failure as a behavioural driver. He actually set out to discover what motivated people to achieve, or how "achievement motivation" or the "need for achievement" developed in children. Yet his experiments are now equally celebrated for their discovery of the opposite dynamic.

Again, detailed by Evans, and following on from earlier experiments by David McClelland, Atkinson (with G.H. Litwin) involved groups of children in reward-based games and activities and recorded that the children approached the tasks in two quite distinct ways: anticipating success or anticipating failure. Atkinson noticed that this divide had an enormous impact on the individual's approach, performance and behaviour during the task.

An individual's attitude (and the outcome) was dictated by whether they had high or low levels of "achievement motivation," concluded Atkinson. Those with high achievement motivation were driven by both their need and their expectation of success. They focused on the reward of task fulfilment and behaved in ways likely to generate success.

Meanwhile, those with low achievement motivation were motivated by a fear of failure, and sought to avoid even moderately difficult tasks due to their expectation of failure. What most concerned them was the *humiliation* of failure – resulting in them employing a series of tactics to either evade the task or disguise their avoidance (which included disrupting the entire task).

Atkinson's discovery forms the key divide in this book, so bears repetition:

- Those with high *achievement motivation* have an expectation of success and are focused on the rewards that success will bring. We shall call them **High-AMs** (although Atkinson's label was the more complex nAch, meaning "need for achievement").
- Those with a high *fear of failure* have an expectation of failure and are focused on avoiding the humiliation failure will bring. We shall call them **High-FFs**.
- The majority of people reading this book will be High-FFs (with a high fear of failure), although it is important to bear in mind that those studying achievement motivation, and its opposite, found a spectrum of responses.

Atkinson was to make one more – extraordinary – discovery. High-FFs had no problem attempting tasks that were deemed very difficult or almost impossible. This was due to the fact the potential humiliation of failure remained low. So while High-AMs chose a challenging but achievable range of tasks in anticipation of success and reward, High-FFs chose only those tasks they were almost certain to complete or almost certain to fail, along with everyone else attempting that task. For instance, Atkinson involved children in a game of throwing hoops on a peg. Those with high achievement motivation (High-AMs) stood a bold but realistic distance from the peg while those with high fear of failure (High-FFs) stood either right on top of the peg, or so far back success was almost impossible.

Task perseverance, task avoidance

Australian psychologist Norman Feather undertook similar experiments and came to similar conclusions – finding a bias in the willingness of subjects to persist in a task they had failed first-time based on their levels of achievement motivation. Those with high levels of achievement motivation (our High-AMs) would tend to persevere at an easy task they failed – perhaps reassessing the difficulty of the task and adding further concentration or determination. Meanwhile, those with a high fear of failure (our High-FFs) were disinclined to continue, wanting to avoid the shame of failing.

Feather also found that he could manipulate the response by presenting the task as easy or difficult. High-FFs were inclined to continue if they were told that the task was difficult because, he concluded, the shame of failing had been lowered. In fact the task he'd been setting his subjects – drawing around a figure without lifting the pen from the paper – was impossible, although at first glance appeared easy.

Summarizing the experiments, Phil Evans contended that levels of achievement motivation played a significant role when it came to "the wisdom of career choices in students." Those with high achievement motivation would choose realistic but challenging careers – perhaps joining a profession or becoming a scientist. They aimed high – avoiding careers with low incentives – but were grounded. They steered clear of pursuing overly ambitious or unrealistic "wildest dreams" such as pop stardom or TV fame.

On the other hand, those with high fear of failure would either keep their career choices at an uninspiring level, or aim for something that would bring either fabulous rewards (such as fame) or, far more likely, failure – although the consequences of failure would be judged kindly simply because success was so unlikely. Indeed, in these circumstances, being seen as a "trier" would be viewed positively.

Mastery or ego orientation

Phil Evans's excellent recounting of the history of experiments studying the emotional drivers for our behaviour was published in the mid 1970s. Yet the research he detailed is backed up in the 1980s by Carol Dweck and Ellen Leggett, also of Stanford University. Their goal-setting experiments concluded that children were either "mastery-oriented" or "ego-oriented" with the mastery-oriented kids (High-AMs in other words) believing not only that they could surmount obstacles and reach a solution but relished the opportunity of doing so.

For mastery-oriented kids, learning or skill-improvement was their focus, meaning they would persist in the face of setbacks, while ego-oriented kids (our High-FFs) were more inclined towards not losing face, so would avoid situations where this was a possibility. Their need for achievement, it seems, was lower than their need to not appear foolish. Of course, for both groups there were major implications for their future academic and career achievement levels as well as their development of life-long learning habits.

So we seem to have a well-known psychological phenomenon on our hands. High-AMs are not worried about the possibility of failure and tend to be stimulated by situations involving some degree of risk. They are more likely to accept challenges where the probability of success is no more than possible, and perceive easy tasks as too boring or beneath them to attempt. Meanwhile, High-FFs fear public humiliation and therefore seek to avoid the potential for failure. They are more likely to attempt only very simple tasks or tasks that are all but impossible simply because they would win credit for trying and it may mask their avoidance of more attainable goals.

Self-help books aimed at High-FFs

Evans's book was aimed at an academic audience, although it produced a strong personal response in me. Secretly, self-denyingly – but absolutely – I was a High-FF. I feared failure and acted accordingly, whether this was with immediate tasks or life choices. This was true in my careers but had a resonance in every aspect of my life and certainly my academic failures as a child.

Phil Evans's book had been published in 1975 (I'd found my copy in a small-town second-hand bookshop) with the experiments on motivation going back to the 1940s. Others had added to the research in the 1980s and 1990s. So why had all those "how to succeed" self-help books I'd devoured over the years not addressed the fundamental issues exposed by the experiments, not least the inappropriate goal-setting of the High-FF?

Indeed, those "how to succeed" books are a major publishing genre occupying miles of shelving (especially in the US). Alain de Botton in *Status Anxiety* (2004) claims they started with Benjamin Franklin's *Autobiography* (1790), which encouraged readers to act through homilies such as "there are no gains without pains" and "early to bed, early to rise. . . ."

William Matthews's 1874 book *Getting On in the World* was the first to attack the subject head on, followed by William Maher's *On the Road to Riches* (1876) and Edwin T. Freedley's *The Secret of Success in Life* (1881). Dale Carnegie's *How to Win Friends and Influence People* (1936) is perhaps the most famous, these days closely followed by Anthony Robbins *Awaken the Giant Within* (1992). And even children's fictional characters have got in on the act: *Winnie the Pooh on Success* by Roger E. Allen and Stephen D. Allen was published in 1998.

Yet every one of these and hundreds of other self-help books are sending a potentially damaging message to those with a high fear of failure – that it's OK to reach for the stars. "Go on, you *can* be a popstar," they seem to be saying before imparting admittedly useful methodologies for goal achievement.

Susan Jeffers in *Feel the Fear and do it Anyway* (1987) at least addresses the core concern. But what if "doing it" wasn't the right thing to do? What if people were setting the wrong goals based on their fear of failure – avoiding, sustainable and obtainable careers in favour of the avoidance-based "wildest dreams" the books seem to encourage? As someone with high fear of failure, what I needed from a self-help book was guidance in developing the evaluation skills of those with high achievement motivation. A book that says: "look, just maybe your entire concept of goal-setting and achievement is flawed and needs rethinking."

Just maybe the answer lies not in "obtaining our highest goal" but in setting goals that are appropriate and lead to fulfilment. Rather than "feeling the fear and doing it anyway" what about recognizing that fear may be leading us in the wrong direction?

Dream fulfilment is a false promise

The AM/FF split is therefore well documented. Yet it appears to have been ignored by much of the modern self-help literature, which – while clearly aimed at frustrated people with an acute fear of failure, or with related issues such as poor confidence – perhaps assumes we would retain our unrealistic and avoidance-based goals even if we could overcome our fears. Meanwhile, those boring High-AMs are already grounded and thus an unlikely market for books on self-improvement.

As a saturated High-FF, however, it dawned on me that it was the dream that needed adjusting. The very idea of dream fulfilment is a false promise for those with fear of failure – potentially even a lie. It is a comfort blanket that, in reality, suffocates personal fulfilment through the idea that it is "all or nothing," so the only high-esteem choice is "all" – the pursuit of which will result in either abject failure or arrogant whooping success that, for insecure High-FFs, generates as many problems as it solves.

Indeed, for the first time I saw celebrity behaviour – the arrogance, the addictions, the inappropriate marriages and affairs, and the wanton self-destruction – as it really is. Many celebrities are High-FFs that by some miracle have hooped the distant peg and are now floundering around in a sea of insecurities. Those with high achievement motivation, meanwhile, are lawyers or accountants or medics or just about anything else that is successful, normal and involves high levels of sustainable self-esteem.

Avoidance behaviours

Yet it wasn't just celebrity behaviour that came into sharp focus thanks to my new-found enlightenment. It was mine. Fear of failure had driven my behaviour since early childhood. I just hadn't previously joined the dots:

Rebelliousness. At nine I led a small gang of shoplifters (eventually caught in *Woolworths*) and indulged in petty-vandalism. With pursed lips, the village mothers discussed my antics, we well as my open rudeness and abuse when challenged, and I was soon banned from many of their homes.

Acting the clown. I could become loud and disruptive in the classroom – causing mayhem for any teacher I perceived as weak. Happy to be the fall guy, making people laugh at my own expense was something I carried into the workplace – a trait which led to my biggest perceived failure of all: my first book (see below).

Feuding/criticizing. Insecure within the group, I was never happier than when someone else was being attacked (sometimes physically). I was delighted to line up against those seen as inadequate – both at school and later at work. And this led to feuding, with me regularly going to war with particular individuals, sometimes for no other reason than the assumption I could win (with me going into full retreat at the first sign of resistance).

Difficulty settling into mainstream activity. My mother enrolled me in the Cub Scouts. I hated it. Football – I fell out with the adults in charge (repeating the exercise when some local men formed a rival team). Judo – again, it didn't last. Even as an adult I've soon absconded from formalized activities: squash, tennis, golf, sailing, residents' associations, even historical re-enactment societies – I started them all thinking it would do me good, and quickly found reasons to stop.

Withdrawal. As a child, I was content to pursue solitary endeavours – my innate creativity (see Part Three) eventually focusing on a wholly imaginary country that occupied my mind into adulthood. It was a scaled-up version of my neighbourhood – in which my village became a city and the local town a metropolis – meaning I could almost constantly indulge myself in this parallel universe.

Superstition. Convinced my fate was in the hands of others (see Bernard Weiner in the next section), I developed an acute interest in tarot-card readings, astrology and the predications of Nostradamus (an interest that lasted into my thirties). This led to a belief in conspiracy theories as well as a major indulgence in the Ouija Board (with anyone I could persuade to join in). But it also led to convictions of poor luck.

Injustice convictions/guilt. It always seemed to be *my* fault – at least that was my perception. Mishaps in the house had a way of connecting back, to the point where any negative event – anywhere – would trigger feelings of guilt and quick-reaction defensiveness, which further raised suspicions.

Fantasy and exaggeration. I've dealt with the solitary fantasies but what about telling my school friends I was Welsh, my university mates I was a born-and-bred Cockney and others that I was Jewish or bisexual or a recovering alcoholic? Of course, I wasn't any of these things. I was a boring white, lower middle-class heterosexual from exurbia – convinced that such a "straight" background would be too boring for others to contemplate.

Dream fulfilment careers. As Atkinson points out, High-FFs shoot for the stars in order to avoid challenging but realistic career choices. For me, that meant becoming a famous writer – even writing a full-length (but appallingly ungrammatical) novel aged 12. Of course, this ambition has never quite gone away.

The above traits – and others such as indecision, exam stress, avoiding promotion, paranoia and even such seemingly confident traits as being overly cool or a political extremist – will be familiar to many High-FFs reading this book. Their connection? They are all forms of avoidance. Many suggest "I won't" to hide an inner conviction that "I can't." We are hiding from our darkest inner perceptions of inadequacy, and our fears that our shortcomings will be humiliatingly revealed.

"Attribution theory" and the "locus of control"

Yet there is one more motivational psychologist worth mentioning. In the late 1980s Bernard Weiner from the University of California published his "attribution theory" to explain the emotional and motivational aspects of academic success and failure.

From Weiner's work it becomes clear that our frame of mind makes a major difference. Those with a positive frame of mind (our High-AMs) attribute their successes to their own abilities. Meanwhile, they attribute their failures to a lack of effort or a need to acquire new skills. And those with a negative frame of mind (our High-FFs) attribute their successes to the fact the task was easy or that they were lucky, and their failures to their innate and unchangeable lack of ability.

Weiner talked of a "locus of control" – a concept first developed by Julian B. Rotter in the 1950s – to explain the extent to which individuals believe they can shape events that have an impact upon them. Having a positive frame of mind, it seems, is based on an "internal locus of control." This results in a self-belief we can adapt or control external factors – or at least their impact upon us. Meanwhile, a negative frame of mind is based on an "external locus of control," which results in a self-belief that we are at the whim of external forces, such as luck or fate or the manipulation of others that we have no power to influence. An external locus of control suggests that our skills (or more likely our lack of them) are innate, which means our ability to learn new skills is limited.

Not only does this suggest a major link between negative self-beliefs and a fear of failure, it brings us right back to the High-FF's impaired evaluation abilities. Those with high achievement motivation ignore the noise around them in favour of their own inner confidence and reasoning – even when evaluating their failures, which they assume are surmountable with new learning and deeper concentration. Meanwhile, those with a high fear of failure assume failures or setbacks are insurmountable because their (presumably low) skill levels are fixed.

And their poor self-beliefs mean that they are subject to any influence or signal – good or bad – from outside. Friends, family, colleagues, teachers, rivals, strangers, gurus, even celebrities and fictional characters: all offer seemingly more credible information about their detailed and particular circumstances and abilities than they can evaluate for themselves, hence making them vulnerable to the big promises of the "you can do it" self-help literature, as well as a reliance on concepts such as luck, fate or astrology.

So poor self-beliefs lead to poor evaluations (based on our fears), which lead to poor responses (also based on our fears): a horrible self-fulfilling vortex of failure. Sounds like you? It certainly sounded like me. Damn that inner doubt that made every positive move seem unsustainable (just temporary luck), while every negative event confirmation of my own inner awfulness. Damn that poor self-belief that was willing to listen to any advice no matter how inappropriate – from no matter what source – while undermining my already fragile inner resolve. And damn the fear of failure that destroyed my academic potential as a child and my career progress as an adult in favour of the easy options or ridiculous dreams.

Case Study 1 – Fearing humiliation

James is a 35-year-old musician who started playing the piano aged two. He showed precocious talent throughout his early years and, encouraged by the adults around him, expected to become a professional. However, aged 12 he attempted to play a piece of music from memory to a large public audience. His mind went blank. He froze, and had to leave the stage feeling utterly humiliated.

This episode not only knocked his confidence, it induced fear-based paralysis whenever tangentially reminded of the event. From then on he always played from music and, over time, began to dread playing in front of an audience.

"Looking back," said James, who contacted me after reading the first edition of *What's Stopping You?* "I can remember experiencing the same maelstrom of negative emotions at each concert: a strong desire to keep proving my worth following the humiliation, coupled with a perhaps irrational fear that I assumed the audience would know the music better than me, and criticize me for every fluffed note."

Eventually, the fear won and James pursued a rather more mundane career outside of music. However, he did return to performing music in front of an audience (he is now the organist at his local church) after attending a "positive-thinking" course arranged through his work.

"I realized that my fear of public humiliation had been dictating both my behaviour and my career choices," he said. "My day-to-day decisions were based on how I perceived other people might react to me, rather than what was in my long-term interest. I was simply trying to save face. But I learnt that I can make positive choices about how I interact with people. If the interaction is constructive, then I can choose to accept and learn from it; if the interaction is unconstructive, then I can choose to ignore it."

What's Stopping You? *You may avoid challenging but achievable tasks due to a fear of public humiliation while having no problem attempting near-impossible tasks because failure will be kindly judged (and they may mask your avoidance of achievable tasks). Unfortunately for those with fear of failure, your career and life choices can follow the same dynamic.*

2

EXTERNAL RESPONSES

In his landmark 1994 book *Emotional Intelligence*, Daniel Goleman describes the instant impact various emotional incidents have on the body. For instance, anger makes blood rush to the hands ready for action. Meanwhile, the heart rate increases and there is a surge of adrenalin. With fear, blood rushes to the skeletal muscles such as the legs, the face blanches and the body momentarily freezes as it decides whether hiding may be a better option than running or fighting. Meanwhile, there is a flood of hormones that puts the body on general alert, making us edgy and incapable of concentrating on anything other than the threat to hand.

Such a response offers obvious short-term advantages – especially if we are truly threatened. However, as Goleman says, someone experiencing these physical responses to an emotional state for any length of time is like a "car stuck in a perpetual high gear," with all the attendant physical damage this implies.

Yet it's the brain's response that causes the more permanent damage. These high-drama moments cause the amygdala – which Goleman describes as a key cluster of components in the limbic system dealing with emotions such as anxiety, distress and fear – to signal other brain regions to strengthen their memory of the incident. This creates a bigger imprint within the memory, which generates a new neural "setpoint" that can cause a lifelong resetting of the brain's default (i.e. instant) responses to even tangentially similar situations – making us respond with fear, perhaps without even realizing why.

"Such traumatic memories seem to remain as fixtures in brain function because they interfere with subsequent learning – specifically, with relearning a more normal response to those traumatizing events," says Goleman.

This is not dissimilar to cases of post-traumatic stress disorder (PTSD). Like Miller's rats, both the memory and the ability to learn have gone awry – a process psychologists call "fear conditioning" in which something that is not threatening is treated as a threat simply because it is immediately associated with the past traumatic event that created the fearful default setting in the brain.

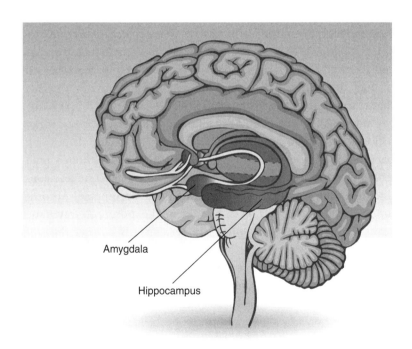

Figure 2.1 The limbic system showing the amygdala and the hippocampus

Equally importantly, the fear response arrives via a "neural hijacking" – an emotional explosion in which the limbic system proclaims an emergency, "recruiting the rest of the brain to its urgent agenda," says Goleman. This hijacking, which is instantaneous and arrives in an emotional surge, overrides what Goleman calls the "thinking brain" – leading to instant emotional responses based on fear, whatever the reality.

Post-traumatic stress disorder

I have no doubt that this is exactly what happens to those with a high fear of failure. Past traumas have hardwired fear into us, generating our own version of PTSD that leads to fear conditioning and fear responses when the memory is triggered. Yale University's Dennis Charney states, in his paper *The Science of Emotion – Understanding PTSD*, that studies have shown that such traumas can occur at a very early age or even in the womb (perhaps passed through the mother), so we may not even be conscious of the events that trigger our own version of PTSD.

And, crucially for High-FFs, trauma in this instance can mean incidents of public humiliation or episodes involving demeaning parents, siblings, teachers or peers. These traumas, although mild in comparison to serious cases of PTSD, can still generate fear conditioning that induces a neural hijacking when prompted. According to studies into PTSD, even brief or mild exposure to traumatic stress – especially when young – can permanently damage the hippocampus (a key part of the brain for the formation of memories), stopping normal new cell growth. This means that we will *always* evaluate information via this fearful default setting, making those neural hijackings – and the associated fear response – inevitable.

And our hormones only add to the problems. Threatening situations or other fear-inducing traumas cause the hormone cortisol to be secreted, the production of which is enormously influenced by our early upbringing.

"In normal people [cortisol] levels go up and down according to what is happening at any given moment," says Oliver James in his influential 2002 book on family survival, *They F*** You Up*, "but if we were living in a highly stressful family in our first six or so years of life [or suffered other stress] this acts like a thermostat, setting our cortisol levels too high or too low in adulthood."

James states that adults who suffered childhood traumas experience damage to their cortisol regulatory system resulting in it either closing down, which can lead to low empathy and callousness, or becoming jammed on permanent alert, which can lead to stress, anger, anxiety and depression.

So can we be rewired to suppress Goleman's neural hijackings or normalize James's cortisol thermostat? Fears can subside over time through natural and spontaneous relearning, says Goleman (citing Charney). For instance, a child once frightened by a dog can lose their fear of that breed through strong positive contact with a similar dog later in life. Yet in many cases the distrust never entirely disappears. PTSD can prevent spontaneous relearning from *ever* occurring.

So profound can be the impact of the trauma that those neural hijackings create a fear response whenever the memory is triggered. In fact, each reminder can add to the trauma – turning childhood fears based on traumatic early-life events into major and paralyzing adult phobias. In many cases the brain never naturally relearns a milder reaction, which means that the learning process is impaired and the fear response can only ever be diverted through intense concentration and active relearning over many years.

Daniel Goleman and high EQ

From reading Goleman and James and other books describing early-life trauma and its impact on the emotions, I became convinced that – perhaps due to traumatic early-childhood events – those with a high fear of failure have impaired emotional responses that are not experienced by those with high achievement motivation. Responses, moreover, that lead to false evaluations, which, in turn, lead to fear-based external responses – themselves leading to poor results that further confirm our fears.

Those with high achievement motivation, meanwhile, are free of such negative and self-fulfilling responses. In fact, High-AMs clearly have what Goleman calls high EQ (i.e. a high "emotional quotient" – comparing it to "intelligence quotient" or IQ). And such emotional competence, according to Goleman, dominates our potential for success in life (he infers by as much as 80 per cent) – creating a major chasm between the achievement potential of those with high-EQ and those with low-EQ.

He lists high-EQ "competencies" as including the ability to self-start, to grasp personality-based politics and to get along with people. Other positive innate high-EQ traits, meanwhile, include a concern for others, self-knowledge, an ability to manage emotions, social adroitness, enthusiasm and commitment.

Of course, this also reads like a list of everything those with a high fear of failure are not. I failed on most of these counts and even those I didn't – such as enthusiasm – could easily be judged as no more than a mask to hide deeply held insecurities.

High-FFs are capable of emotional intelligence

Emotional intelligence (or high-EQ) is therefore vital if we want to make the move towards achievement motivation. Those with fear of failure need to develop skills in all the above areas, which seems daunting although is far from impossible. We may be High-FFs, with all the resulting baggage, but we *are* capable of emotional intelligence, however innate our fears and insecurities. We simply need to learn it. Broken down into constituent parts, each of Goleman's traits is an attainable goal for the High-FF.

- *Ability to self-start* – self-starting is little more than having direction (see Part Two), knowing how to take that first step (see Part Three) and how to keep going despite the setbacks. High-FFs need help in this respect, but help is at hand.
- *To grasp personality-based politics* – good people judgement comes from being aware of your own emotions and your own and others' objectives (see Part Four). It also comes from being strongly goal-oriented and with the emotional maturity to genuinely seek win–win outcomes. Certainly, if we are meeting our own objectives, we can help others meet theirs, and the politics subsides (although, as we shall see, sustainable progress may mean reversing the order in which this is achieved).
- *To get along with people* – many High-FFs have poor people skills, but remove the classic frustrations suffered by those with a high fear of failure and our evaluations of others should improve, making our dealings with people a lot easier (see Part Four).
- *To be concerned for others* – ditto. High-AMs can afford to be more charitable, we feel, but so can we once we have developed strong principles-centred goals and are making good progress.
- *Self knowledge* – we are rapidly acquiring this, thanks.
- *Ability to manage emotions* – aware that those neural hijackings are based on flawed evaluations and incorrect assumptions, we can learn to create better second responses based on more positive evaluations – hopefully closer in time to the actual neural-hijacking moments. That monkey won't disappear, but we can negate the potential damage he causes.
- *Social adroitness* – another innate gift for those with high achievement motivation that we can learn. There is no social skill beyond the High-FF once we have self-awareness, are goal-oriented and have learnt some tactics and habits for motivation, task-processing and people management.
- *Enthusiasm and commitment* – no longer a mask if we are travelling the right path and making good progress towards the right goals.

Getting on top of our external responses

Our number one concern at this stage, however, is to get on top of our external responses to those neural hijackings. These are the key moments that disable those with high fear of failure – leaving us emotionally distraught and mentally derailed. Our external responses are the symptoms of our fear of failure and it is here where we should concentrate our first line of attack (or at least self-awareness). Whether those neural hijackings generate anger, frustration, anxiety or depression, these are the responses that produce many of the poor self-fulfilling results for those with a high fear of failure.

But if we can understand what we are feeling, and why, we may be able to start the process of creating better second responses and therefore begin to undermine those self-fulfilling behavioural changes caused by the triggering of our fears. This is unlikely to be easy, and nothing below is written flippantly. Yet self-awareness can help turn our thinking in a more positive direction, which will hopefully – in time and with many small confirming steps – change those external responses.

Perhaps the easiest external response to understand is the most extreme: anger. Anger is fear's ugly sister, so while fear remains the hidden Cinderella, its noisy sibling is out and proud and extremely menacing. As emotions go, anger is by far the most apparent, as well as the most destructive. Not only do we lose control over our feelings, we lose control over our actions – sometimes destroying strong, long-term, constructive activity in seconds.

"No other emotion – anxiety, depression, even love – erases our control so completely," write health practitioner Carl Semmelroth and psychologist Donald E.P. Smith in *The Anger Habit* (2000).

And anger goes way beyond pure rage. As Semmelroth and Smith note, critical thoughts, revenge fantasies and paranoid interpretations of others' behaviour can all provide the context for anger, whether we outwardly boil-over, show irritation or inwardly seethe.

Anger as concealment and control

One route to overcoming anger is to understand its purpose. Anger is often an act of concealment, a way of hiding our inner feelings of guilt or confusion or hurt or – most likely – fear.

As US family counsellor Carol D. Jones writes in her 2004 book *Overcoming Anger*: "It's just plain easier to tell yourself you're mad [i.e. angry] than it is to say you're sad, confused, hurt or frightened."

That's a powerful admission and one likely to chime with many High-FFs: it's not anger, stupid, it's fear.

And the fact that anger is mostly an external manifestation is a clue to its other core purpose. According to *The Anger Habit*, anger is often an attempt to control others. The angry person perceives that they are in a contest for power, and they are losing (hence the fear). Things are not falling into place as they had hoped, so they are trying to change the situation through coercion.

"Anger tells us that we are preparing to force others, or ourselves, to comply with some expectation," it concludes.

Both *The Anger Habit* and *Overcoming Anger* focus on awareness and acceptance as the key ingredients for overcoming anger. Angry people must accept that the root cause of their anger is not the other person's behaviour but their own negative self-beliefs. It is their inner feelings of fear and inadequacy that they are raging against.

Meanwhile, the godfather of motivational gurus, Anthony Robbins, goes a little easier on anger. In *Awaken the Giant Within* (1992) he sees anger, like other emotions, as an "action signal." Anger can be a positive, he claims, if we "turn that emotional intensity into directed excitement and passion." Many angry people feel locked in a cycle of fear and frustration, with their anger demonstrating their clear desire to unlock the cage and get going in a more rewarding direction. The motivation is there, but rattling the cage won't get us on our way. We need to find a key. And that takes planning (see Part Two).

Frustration and anxiety

Of course this brings us neatly to frustration, anger's little brother. Anthony Robbins also has a lot to say about frustration. He sees it as an exciting action signal because frustration actually comes from a sense of inner self-belief that we could and should be in a better place. It says the solution is within range but that we need to change our approach. In this respect frustration is very different to disappointment, which is a more final feeling – of negative acceptance – that we are defeated and will never attain what we seek.

Anxiety, meanwhile, is less easily dismissed and is, in fact, a symptom of PTSD – a long-term reaction to the continual triggering of the fear response. As we have seen, such triggering leads to avoidance of situations in which we may be triggered, with anxiety the response to even the prospect of such situations. Yet, according to Glen R. Schiraldi in *The Post-Traumatic Stress Disorder Sourcebook* (2000), anxious people can become conditioned to fear even the tactics or distractions they use to avoid the fear response.

For instance, the earlier child frightened by the dog may become anxious at even the prospect of contacting a similar dog – maybe in a park or along a footpath – perhaps changing her route to school because of it, with even the new route eventually triggering anxiety because of its association with the original trauma. And it takes no great leaps to apply such anxiety-based behaviour to the avoidance tactics of Atkinson's High-FF children.

Reversing this self-fulfilling cycle of fear and worry is no mean feat, and usually involves professional help. But, as Schiraldi states, we can learn to confront our anxieties through the acceptance of our condition and, through therapy, the erection of protective "boundaries" as well as the avoidance of "retraumatizing behaviours" (such as alcohol).

And we can also take tiny steps towards a less anxious future, perhaps learning over time to reframe our concerns by focusing on the positive, by not trying to right past wrongs (revenge fantasies stoke-up rather than reduce anxiety) and by forcing objective evaluations onto any anxiety-inducing situation (hopefully closer in time to the situation itself) – all as recommended by Dale Carnegie, one of the most famous self-improvement writers of the twentieth century in *How to Stop Worrying and Start Living* (1948).

Depression is a thief

Which brings us to depression: "Depression is a thief that steals from people, robbing them of energy, vitality, self-esteem and any pleasure that they might previously have enjoyed," writes Irish psychologist Tony Bates in *Understanding and Overcoming Depression* (2001).

Depression is typified by an unrelenting sad mood, an absence of energy, problems concentrating or remembering, a loss of interest in activities once enjoyed, and difficulties with sleeping and eating. In many ways it is the flipside to anger – an emotional response based on feelings of defeat and withdrawal, making anger seem like a positive fighting response in comparison.

Yet Bates's recommendations for treating depression strike a chord with our programme for aiding those with fear of failure. Awareness of the root causes – such as negative early-life experiences or harsh, demeaning or controlling parents or other sown seeds for low self-esteem – is a major step, as well as knowledge of the destructive thought patterns that spiral into depression. We can attack these with deliberate attempts to reframe our thoughts more positively, he states, and by taking small actionable steps that slowly lift the clouds.

"Recovery from depression is a journey rather than a destination," says Bates, echoing the sentiments of this book on both fear of failure and low self-esteem.

Yet Robbins is more forthright on depression – holding the depressed person responsible for his or her condition.

"In order to be depressed," he says in his seminal work *Unlimited Power* (1987), "you have to view your life in specific ways."

It takes effort to do this, he states, involving what we say to ourselves and in what tone. It also involves how we hold ourselves and how we breathe. And it involves playing games with our blood-sugar levels through poor diet and excessive alcohol.

"Some people have created this state so often though, that it is easy to produce," says Robbins – pointing out that to many it can actually feel like the most comforting state to be in, helped by secondary gains such as sympathy from others and allowances from peers. But we had to work at getting ourselves into such a bad place, he says, just as we can and should work to get ourselves out of it.

Taking responsibility

Far from being callous, Robbins's tough-love approach hits upon an important concept for any High-FF hoping to develop achievement motivation. We need to take responsibility for our thoughts and actions, as well as our emotional and external responses, no matter how they manifest themselves. This is a theme that runs right through the motivational universe and is something we *must* grasp, not least because any form of progress is impossible if we continue to blame others (parents, siblings, peers, teachers) for who we are and how we respond.

Whatever your personal history, no one else is responsible for *your* actions and *your* behaviour, or even *your* inner thoughts, evaluations and responses. *You* are. Blame is simply an excuse for inaction. Meanwhile, taking responsibility is the quickest route for turning those feelings of fear, frustration, anger or depression into better responses.

In *The Seven Habits of Highly Effective People* (1989), Stephen Covey makes it clear that anyone seeking self-improvement needs to take complete responsibility for their responses in every situation. In probably the most important statement in what is *the* most influential self-help book in this area, Covey writes "it isn't what happens to us that counts, it's how we respond."

He actually wrote "between stimulus and response man has the freedom to choose" but it is such a vital concept, I thought it important to put it in language that would help us remember it (Covey also wrote "in choosing our response to circumstances, we powerfully affect our circumstances," which is equally memorable).

In other words, we may not be responsible for the external forces that intrude upon our lives – or, indeed, for what generated our self-beliefs in early childhood – but as adults, we are 100 per cent responsible for our evaluation of such forces, as well as the impact we allow them to have upon us and, most importantly, our responses.

The answer is not to deny responsibility (or "response-ability" as Covey prefers to construct it) by blaming others and circumstances. The answer is to embrace it. Taking responsibility for our past failures and current predicaments – and even our feelings – is a fantastically liberating concept. Just imagine – if you are totally responsible for where you find yourself today, even in terms of how you feel inwardly: awful as that may seem – discomforting as it is – it is also wonderfully empowering. It means *you* are totally responsible for your future. It is in *your* hands.

Focus on the present and future

Taking responsibility is a giant leap towards achievement motivation – regaining Weiner's "locus of control" even if the current self-view is a negative one (Covey also stresses that we may have to accept a negatively assessed starting point). Another is to recognize something equally important – that everything up until the moment we read this sentence is in the past. *And that we cannot change the past.*

"Put the past in the past and focus on the present," said Dale Carnegie (1948). In fact he wrote "shut out the yesterdays which have lighted fools the way to dusty death," but such prose can be off-putting to modern readers.

Carnegie blamed the past – and obsessing about past mistakes – as one of the central causes of worry in people. It is also a core reason why the monkey on our shoulder always has the last word – citing past failures as evidence that the future will be no different.

Yet the monkey is lying because he couldn't possibly know. Just as the past cannot be changed, the future cannot be known. So we can choose to approach the future with fear – by listening to the monkey – or we can decide that the past is only relevant as a learning tool for the present and future.

By, first, taking responsibility for our actions and emotions and, second, accepting that we cannot change anything from the past, we have indeed taken control of our present, which is a pretty liberating thought.

Case Study 2 – Replaying past pain

Isobel is dyslexic, although it was only diagnosed in adulthood. Mostly, she'd been the problem youngest child of a large middle-class family – always struggling, always a little alienated (from her teachers, peers and siblings), always a little behind the curve. Yet the family had strong educational values, resulting in her being privately tutored through her A-levels in order to make it to a good university.

Perhaps inevitably, she flunked her degree, although did eventually succeed on a craft-based course at a small Welsh college. For a time, it seemed Isobel had found her thing – working with jewellery as a skilled and independent artisan.

Yet her organizational challenges prevented her making the most of her skills, and she ultimately lapsed into working for others on a casual basis, although regular fall-outs meant these rarely lasted more than a few months.

Eventually she used a small legacy to buy a studio space she could rent to others – slowly expanding her empire with borrowings and further legacies. She now runs studio space for a range of craftspeople and, while still struggling with the disadvantages of her condition, at least manages to support herself as she single-handedly raises two children.

Over time, however, Isobel's resentment with her family has also grown.

She resented the fact her dyslexia was not picked up in childhood, meaning that she felt condemned as inadequate almost from the start. She resented the "persecution" she experienced at the hands of her older siblings, who made no allowances despite the considerable age gap between her and the next youngest. And she resented her parents' laxity with respect to her upbringing – not caring about her mental well-being, despite their concerns regarding her educational attainment.

And this led Isobel to contact me after reading *What's Stopping You?*

In fact, she wanted to dispute one of the book's central tenets.

"How can I take responsibility when others refuse to acknowledge their own?" she wrote. "With my parents, I get angry with them because they cannot see what happened. I end up shouting, and then have to apologize. It happens over and over again, because they won't acknowledge the damage done in my childhood – and the impact it has today. So there has never been any closure."

"There won't be," I wrote back, "And you'll waste your life waiting. Your whole existence will be a re-run of your childhood in the hope of getting a better result." I was speaking from strong personal experience on this one. "If you face the past there will always be something to anger you, which will disable your present. So your best hope is to understand the past, accept it, and face the future – using the past purely as a learning tool."

She wrote back and thanked me, but my guess is that Isobel will be battling this one for a while yet. That said, she's found great joy with her own family and wrote that she was determined to love and nurture her children in ways she thought she'd missed in her own upbringing. And this was perhaps the most effective way for Isobel to use her past experience to achieve a better result, although I still encouraged her to seek help in terms of accepting her own history.

> **What's Stopping You?** *"Fear conditioning" triggers "neural hijackings" that generate fearful responses. Such conditioning may have developed from early-life traumas. To make progress, you must accept this and take total responsibility for your responses when triggered.*

3

FAILURE AS A POSITIVE EXPERIENCE

Any focus on fear of failure needs to look closely at the *fear* of failure – the fact our dread of failure is so powerful it disables our actions. So can failure ever be viewed as nothing to fear? In fact, can it ever be viewed positively? The answer is yes, if that's how we decide to view it. View it as a milestone or lesson on the way to success, then that's what it will be. View it, meanwhile, as a final result and therefore a condemnation of our character and – indeed – that too will be the near-certain result.

My writing "career" is a strong case in point with respect to the self-fulfilling nature of our view of failure. Having spent the last 18 months of my banking career "reverse commuting" to Greenwich, Connecticut, I used the journey to write about my experiences as a single British lad living in New York. Typed up in the evenings, soon I had around 60,000 words and was looking for a literary agent. By some miracle (in fact good research and hard lobbying) I landed one of the most respected literary agents in the business, and she landed me a publishing deal with one of the UK's largest and most respected publishers.

I was set for a career wandering the globe as a humorous writer. I had hooped the distant peg, and whooped around my Upper Westside apartment like a man whose life had changed forever. And while from this distance such a prospect looks a bit silly, the joke wasn't entirely on me. Both the agent and the publisher said the book sold well, although I was disappointed it hadn't sold in its hundreds of thousands. In fact, that was a key reason for my failure with respect to my book-writing career – I understood nothing of the book-publishing world so had no way to gauge my expectations.

Failure is a question of interpretation

Ultimately, I failed as a writer because that's how I decided to view it. By all accounts, a major house publishing my autobiographical first-book while I was still in my early 30s was a strong first step as an author. Sure, it hadn't sold as many as I'd hoped but there were some strong lessons to learn regarding marketing such a book, as well as making sure the publisher is fully onside with respect to distribution – and, indeed, with respect to ensuring the author has realistic expectations regarding sales.

But I dismissed this in favour of the view that it was a total failure, because it failed to "breakthrough" and turn me into an overnight Nick Hornby. With no fame on offer I opted for the monkey's interpretation that its failure to make headlines was a final confirmation of my innate awfulness. As for the lessons, what was the point of them? They'd never be implemented because I'd blown my *only* chance at making it.

And such feelings changed my behaviour – rendering me incapable of rationality when dealing, first, with the publisher, and then with the agent – not helped by an inevitable dose of writer's block for a second book (inevitable because the confidence with which I'd written the original book had evaporated). Before long I'd been thrown out of the author's club altogether.

Of course, I realize now that my behaviour had been that of a classic High-FF. Someone with high achievement motivation would have taken time to consolidate the achievement by controlling the marketing, cultivating the right people and deeply researching the next topic. This was no more than a debut book, the content of which should reflect my values for a future writing career (not the publisher's – who may have a very different idea of the book's potential audience). And if it failed to make the bestseller's list? Well it was a lot to ask for a first book and there are lessons to get me further up the ladder next time.

Those with a high fear of failure, however, react with amazement at the prospect of success and immediately develop inappropriate and undermining behaviour (such as arrogance or boastfulness) while, in reality, losing control of the project and therefore the direction it will take them. And the second the results fail to match our probably-unrealistic expectations, we collapse – condemning ourselves as a fool for having ever thought we could aim so high. We are crap people, we conclude, forever-condemned to our lowly status – not realizing that we have chosen this response from the range of conclusions on offer, some of which were far from condemning.

The link with low self-esteem

While the above interpretation of failure is, as stated, the classic view of the High-FF, it also reveals another personality trait that cannot be ignored when dealing with fear of failure: low self-esteem. Of course, fear of failure and low self-esteem are different afflictions: fear of failure undermines our actions (changing our behaviour), while low self-esteem distorts our beliefs (generating negative evaluations). But, like fear of failure, low self-esteem is a self-fulfilling condition – leading us to evaluate the world in ways that encourage its external confirmation (that we are worthless).

While not all High-FFs have low self-esteem (or *vice versa*), fear of failure and low self-esteem are inextricably and obviously linked. They are fellow travellers – afflictions that feed off each other as much as they feed off their host – meaning that any programme for progress for High-FFs that ignores low self-esteem leaves a gaping and unbridgeable hole in the road.

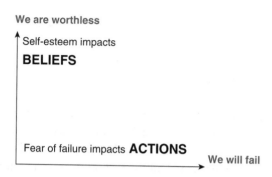

Figure 3.1 There is a major connection between fear of failure and low self-esteem

As with fear, feelings of low self-esteem stem from our experiences from a very young age but are reinforced by what we are told and what we experience, and how we interpret such information, as we become adults. Such feedback – as well as the unconditional love and acceptance (or otherwise) from parents, teachers, siblings and peers – form our inner beliefs, perceptions, conclusions and predictions for life.

Of course, such self-beliefs can be a distortion. According to John Caunt in his very practical 2003 book *Boost Your Self Esteem*, no one is an unbiased observer of themselves. Misrepresentations, omissions and exaggerations can all distort our self-beliefs, resulting in low self-esteem when the same information – presented differently – could have generated entirely different conclusions. In fact many highly successful people suffer from low self-esteem, dismissing their achievements as worthless while ignoring the fact observers may be in awe of those very accomplishments.

"There is no automatic link between one's competence and the level of one's self-esteem," writes Caunt.

Our lives are shaped not by events, says Caunt, but by our responses to those events (echoing Covey), "and the way we respond will be largely dictated by our self-beliefs."

But we *can* change our beliefs, believes Caunt. We have developed one set of beliefs and have given them importance, so we can do the same thing again. We can create our own reality – even manipulating our thoughts, says Caunt. So far in our life we have manipulated them negatively to generate low self-esteem. So why not manipulate them for a more positive purpose?

Reframing failure

Yet this is easier said than done in my view. Hardwired or default settings mean that any newly imposed thoughts or beliefs will feel like they are going against the grain, which will result in setbacks or failures being judged as confirmations that the original settings were the correct ones. That monkey won't shift so easily I'm afraid.

But I may be taking Caunt too literally. What if we tried to reframe negative influences, not to change our inner beliefs or default settings but in order to soften or even alter their impact and therefore potentially change our response? We will look at reframing the negative assumptions that underline low self-esteem in Part Four but what about failure? Can we reframe our view of failure – perhaps even rethinking failure as something to embrace as a necessary part of the journey? Would that change the way we view failure – maybe even helping to reduce our fear of it? Maybe even helping me see the collapse of my writing career in a better light?

Maybe. As we have seen, those paralyzed by fear of failure go to great lengths to avoid public humiliation, including avoiding tasks or careers that may mean contact with the consequences of failure. But, as Alain de Botton says in *Status Anxiety*, fear of failure would not be so great if failure were not so harshly viewed. The world is unsympathetic to failure, referring to those that fail as "losers" – a word, according to de Botton "callously signifying both that people have lost and that they have at the same time forfeited any right to sympathy for having done so."

Depersonalizing failure

This is tough, but is it true? At a primary level, yes of course. We all have to secretly hide our inner joy at even a friend's misfortunes. And with our enemies and rivals we don't even hide it. How many dinner parties have been dominated by the delighted chatter of negative gossip about a mutual acquaintance?

Such *schadenfreude* is classic competitive behaviour that any primatologist (those that study primates) would understand. Yet while this may suggest we have the wrong friends, it is more likely to suggest that we are looking at failure too personally. Exchange personal failure for company or organizational failure and attitudes change considerably. This is because companies are not people. They are a collection of people and machines brought together for an – often highly specialized – common goal.

In other words they are a project. And the failure of a project may dent the reputation and even the self-esteem of those involved. But it is by no means a final and fatal condemnation of the people – just of the project itself. The people involved just start again, a little bruised, a little wiser, but certainly not forever-condemned.

And if we could look at individual failure this way perhaps the crushing enormity and finality of it can be reduced. While not eliminating the pain, surely we can reduce the extent to which a single or series of setbacks confirms our poor self-beliefs? Those with high fear of failure view any failure as absolute, as a confirmation of their personal and irreversible lack of aptitude. But if they could view their progress as a project – and failure as no more than a single setback along the project's path (a bend in the road perhaps) – they may be able to look beyond the pain, or at least not be derailed by it.

For instance, the loss of my writing career was only a "loss" because I chose to treat it as such. Those with high achievement motivation would have seen publication as a strong first step, with further thought required for "that difficult second book" – not its "failure" as an irretrievable condemnation of my abilities as a book writer. Indeed, they would have learnt the lessons, realizing that the initial project was clearly flawed but book writing as a long-term career choice was far from dead (I'd won over two of the most respected literary institutions in London, after all). It was my negative self-beliefs that made it final.

Despite what High-FFs think, failure is never absolute. According to Anthony Robbins, as long as a person breathes and is willing to act, there is nothing final about failure. So why should it be so personal? Is it not just one result, brought about by a range of circumstances some of which were beyond our control?

Seeing failure this way is a difficult task for High-FFs because it tells us to develop the mind of the High-AM, who is willing to learn from negative experiences and make small adjustments in the knowledge that goal attainment is not only possible but probable – even inevitable. They don't need to depersonalize failure because they will not view it personally in the first place. Why should they when they know success is within their grasp?

But High-FFs need tools to get to this point, of which developing a mental depersonalization of their progress, or otherwise, could be one. If we could think of ourselves as companies – as *Me Inc.* or *Me Ltd* rather than just *me* – and our progress as a project, then we should be able to put failures in their place: as mere setbacks rather than ultimate condemnations of our self-worth.

Company failure is a transformed concept

And failure from the perspective of a company is a transformed concept. Tom Peters is perhaps the best known company guru of all. In his well-known book *In Search of Excellence* (written with Robert H. Waterman Jr. in 1982) he quotes senior industry figures such as the heads of Johnson & Johnson and engineering giant Emerson extolling not just the benefits of failure but its absolute requirement as an experience for leadership.

In fact, finding successful company executives promoting the virtues of failure is easy. They all seem to love talking about it:

"Success is not built on success. It's built on failure. It's built on frustration. Sometimes it's built on catastrophe," wrote Sumner Redstone, majority owner of MTV, CBS, Dreamworks, Paramount Pictures.

Meanwhile, Soichiro Honda, founder of Honda Motor Company, said: "Success is 99% failure."

There are hundreds of such quotes.

Some of the most innovative companies even build failure into their business model. According to Tom Peters 3M (inventors of the *Post-it Note* and much else besides) guarantees product managers the ability to run with their inventions backed up by a commitment to total job security should it fail.

And in his seminar-turned-book *Crazy Times Call for Crazy Organizations* (1994) Tom Peters furthers his theme by railing at those bosses that cringe at the thought of failure while celebrating those that embrace it.

On Richard Branson he quotes his publisher John Brown: "The whole secret of Branson's success is his failures . . . He keeps opening things and a good many of them fail – but he doesn't give a f*** – he keeps on going."

Failing is not the problem, according to Tom Peters – far from it. Failure is absolutely necessary. It is *fear* of failure that is the principal cause of paralysis in companies, whether it is the receptionist or the CEO. To overcome this he recommends that companies adopt a culture of failure. Of course this is fine for small failures but that is not enough for Peters. Every now and again the failure has to be "big, bold, embarrassing, face-losing and public." Companies that do not make utter fools of themselves from time to time have become smug, according to Peters, and have therefore stopped growing.

"Fail better"

And while this is a more difficult thing for individuals to accept, it should at least allow us to keep going after experiencing a setback – allowing us to focus on learning the lesson while retaining our focus on the ultimate goal. The most commonly used quote at this point involves Thomas Edison's attempts to invent something (it ranges from the light bulb to synthetic rubber).

"I have not failed," he says after so many unsuccessful attempts at his invention. "I've just found 10,000 ways that won't work."

This chimes with Anthony Robbins in *Unlimited Power*. He states that there are no failures in life – there are only results. If the result was not what we wanted, we should learn from the experience and make better decisions in the future. Indeed, this adds an important caveat to Tom Peters. It says that failure for its own sake – while refreshing – is pointless. The point is to learn from failure. To plunge in, make mistakes, recognize the mistake, learn and try again.

To offer another over-used quote – this time from Samuel Beckett in *Worstward Ho* (1983): "Ever tried. Ever failed. No matter. Try again. Fail again. Fail better."

The key is not to seek failure but to not fear it: to embrace failure, even personal failure, as part of the journey.

This is an important realization for those with a high fear of failure. Not only are setbacks in many cases self-fulfilling due to our fear of failure and the corresponding changes in behaviour this brings, when setbacks do occur – as they will – we must condition ourselves to accept that they are by no means final. They are a result, but not *the* result. In fact, they are still probably a good result, as we can learn the lesson, regroup, and do it again with greater wisdom ("fail better" indeed).

Such setbacks only condemn us as bad people – as being innately awful – if that's how we decide to interpret them. They are only final if we blow the whistle for full-time ourselves. But it's our whistle. We can blow it when we like.

Case Study 3 – The endless apprenticeship

Dermot is a drama teacher near Dublin. Yet his horizons go well beyond the large (and respected) state school where he ploughs his trade. He is also involved in amateur dramatics and has even been involved in productions for one of the city's main theatres.

"Being a playwright is my thing," he said to me when we met. "I've written lots and lots of plays. I get up very early to write, and have become better and better over the years. Many professionals have read my work and thought it had significant merit. And I even managed to persuade the AmDram society I was involved with to put on one of my plays."

Indeed, he wrote the play especially for the group to perform, although that's where the problems started for Dermot. It won only mediocre reviews from a local press that "doesn't do bad reviews" and some of the actors complained afterwards that it was "over written."

Dermot's self-confessed response had been to become defensive: angry even.

"There were some big fallouts, so I left the group and have yet to join another," he said. "Ultimately, I saw it as their fault and reacted badly. But the play *wasn't* over written. They just weren't up to it."

The play had depth, he claimed – although that had turned into a further division with the group, who'd been keener on farce.

"The production before mine was a farce, and the one after mine was going to be a farce, so I thought a change of atmosphere would work, but apparently not," said Dermot. "And there was plenty of humour in my play – it was just a little darker."

I asked if there were other societies that may be interested in more philosophical works, along the Samuel Beckett lines he cited as a major influence.

"I found one that had previously put on a Beckett play," he said. "But they were only interested in Beckett, or other famous Irish playwrights, so they refused to consider my work."

"Could you not work with them first to get yourself established?" I enquired.

Yet the idea of starting again frustrated Dermot. His determination to become a playwright was laudable, but he saw success as a sensational breakthrough moment rather than an incremental process. In his view, he just had to keep writing until he wrote his masterpiece.

I partly agreed with this, and was telling him the story of James Dyson, who made over 5000 versions of his *Dual Cyclone* vacuum cleaner – each with a tiny adjustment. He nodded away in empathy, but nodded less as I described Dyson's 10-year battle to get the appliance to market – including being rejected by nearly all the major manufacturers, as well as legal battles over patents.

"I *did* serve my apprenticeship," he said defensively, as if I'd accused him of not having the fight to keep battling. "But it was with the wrong group so I was wasting my time."

"Not if the next group is the right one," I said, "and with your experience in the first group used as a lesson for getting you nearer your goal next time?"

"I'm a drama teacher," he snapped. "Why do I need to serve *any* form of apprenticeship with amateurs? They should be listening to me, not me to them."

With his anger showing, we changed the subject, although Dermot's defensiveness mellowed by the end of our meeting. He was even beginning to see a way through – perhaps working with the Beckett-focused group on adaptations. It was at least worth a try, I said.

"I guess it all counts as experience," he said as we parted.

What's Stopping You? *You may have a tendency to interpret temporary setbacks as a final condemnation. Yet failure is only final if you judge it so. Most failures are in fact positive learning experiences that can lead to strong progress. Depersonalization is an important tool for helping you to realize this.*

4

PRODUCING BETTER RESPONSES

The UK's NHS is a big beast of a health service, although I doubt its founders considered it would one day be a major resource for attacking low self-esteem in the good citizens of Great Britain and Northern Ireland. Yet, extraordinarily, that's where I found myself not long after my humiliating and drawn out failure as a writer: in counselling sessions in, of all places, a London sexual health clinic.

In their wisdom, some of the more innovative NHS Trusts had realized that many sexual health problems arise from behaviours stemming from self-esteem issues, especially amongst the young. They reasoned that, while those with high self-esteem are having stable relationships with clear long-term goals in mind (even if there is a periodic change of long-term partner), those with low self-esteem pursue low-grade sexual gratification with as many partners as possible, which – as often as not – ultimately involves a trip to the clinic.

And while my own route to the sessions was more tangential, there I sat in one-to-one sessions discussing my poor childhood relationship with my father, as well as the trauma of my family splitting in two when I was a 10-year-old boy. This event, I realized from my chats with the female counsellor, left me with a lifelong fear of rejection from both senior figures (representing my father) and peers (representing my sister, who had also high-tailed it with dad).

Cognitive behavioural therapy

The sessions soon ran their course and my benign cuddle from the NHS had to give way to something more constructive. I was offered a programme on cognitive behavioural therapy (CBT), which seemed to be where the counsellor was heading from early on. As the name suggests, CBT is a behavioural methodology for linking our thoughts, our feelings and our actions to try and generate more positive outcomes. For people with anxiety, depression, panic, phobias, stress and PTSD many NHS Trusts have become keen on prescribing some form of CBT.

CBT works through breaking down problems into thoughts, emotions, physical feelings and actions, and by trying to turn unhelpful perceptions of each into more helpful ones. The literature I was given used an example of being blanked by an acquaintance in the street. The unhelpful route went something like this: thoughts (I was ignored so am not liked); emotions (rejection, sadness, loss of confidence); physical feelings (low energy, depression, sickness); actions (avoidance, isolation).

Meanwhile, the helpful version went something like this: thoughts (he/she seemed distracted so something must be wrong); emotions (concern); physical feelings (none); actions (contact the person to check they are OK).

As you can probably guess I didn't attend the course. Why? I reasoned that it was time I could better use, it was all a bit touchy-feely, and that – going by the example above – I'd be spending my time with assorted under-employed undesirables. I'd enjoyed my sessions with the counsellor but surely things had not got so bad that I'd fall back on state-sponsored therapy?

Of course, the above response is outrageously inappropriate. It is also a classic High-FF avoidance tactic for something that was clearly going to be challenging. I feared failure at CBT and, therefore, avoided it – inventing an excuse that would protect my self-esteem. If I'd genuinely felt the above I could have found private therapy sessions for angst-ridden professionals or even seen if the counsellor was prepared to help me offline from the NHS.

Start a diary

The CBT literature, however, contained one nugget that was to transform my perceptions and evaluations overnight. It was a bullet point tucked away on an inside page under the heading: *CBT – the work*. It stated that "the therapist may ask you to keep a diary, to help identify patterns and thoughts, emotions, physical feelings and actions."

This was a coincidence as – fed up with being in a bad or depressed mood – I'd wondered whether my moods were altered by my diet and had started jotting down notes in a page-per-week diary sent by a supplier. Soon, I was testing my moods against the time of day, days of the week, seasons and even the phases of the moon (easy in the better diaries). And, before long, I was no longer just writing "mood" but adding descriptions such as "self-loathing" or "irritation."

Yet the CBT documents were suggesting a whole new level of journal-keeping – recording what I was feeling, as well as why I felt this way and how I was responding. I bought an A5 page-per-day diary and started writing it all down. I quickly became addicted. I found that recording my moods helped to rationalize them. My neural hijackings – while still frequent and unwelcome – seemed to dissipate almost as soon as I'd started writing, although the pen indentations on the page still attest to the state I was sometimes in.

And I also noticed from my furtive loiterings in the self-help sections of bookshops that just about every self-help book told me to keep a diary or journal. Some were stricter than others in what they required recording but many seemed to include versions of the following:

Moods: any episodes of anger, depression, frustration, hurt. The aim is to be as explicit as possible and to record your feelings at the time. So if you felt something like: "that Johnson's done it again – he's stolen my idea the totally brainless idiot who couldn't have a single unique thought of his own but will probably end up my boss *arrrgghhhhhh*," then that's what you write down.

Having said this, it may also help to leave a space under it for a more reflective comment. This could range from "it turns out Johnson told the boss it was my idea. He is a good guy, so why was my first reaction so angry?" to "I need to get Johnson onside. My feelings towards him are irrational and undermining me – my move" to "I'm still angry about this but thank God the anger only appeared here and wasn't shouted across the entire fifth floor."

Obstacles: "No matter how prepared you are," says Anthony Robbins, "you are going to hit a few rocks along the river of life." The diary is the place to record these rocks and try and formulate a way around them. Just writing problems down can create a clarity-of-thought that removes the emotional clutter.

Goals: we'll come to the big stuff in Part Two but the day-to-day diary is for the small stuff. What's the next step? What's the time-frame? Who do I call to work out what the next step is? In fact this is the most important aspect of the diary – making your diary the key tool for recording those small, positive, victory-by-victory building blocks of achievement. As stated, High-FFs need to create a map to chart their progress. *Your diary is that map.*

Results: how did the next step go? Did the call get the result you wanted? Yes, how come? What's next? No, why? What went wrong? Again, what's next?

Controlling displacement activity: I used to record my alcohol units. Then I realized I was drinking too much and used the diary to record progress towards keeping my intake to my weekly limit. When this kept failing I gave up drinking and now put a zero in that corner every day. Too much time on the internet or watching TV is also recorded – again with an admonishment.

Self-flagellation: anyone reading my diary (heaven forbid – this is the most private of documents) would be shocked at how hard I am on myself. Yet that's the point. People with fear of failure beat themselves up all the time. I'm not asking you to stop beating yourself up – just that you do it constructively. Any beatings need to involve a "lessons learnt" element as well as practical next steps.

Self-congratulation: but also record the triumphs. I use a tick system to note what I am pleased with. The creation of new, more positive, neural pathways in the brain involves tiny steps taken in the right direction. Over time, this will build your confidence and move you towards a better place. It's an exciting journey but it *must* be recorded if the steps taken are to lead anywhere sustainable.

Experiences: I love rereading my diary from my wedding day, or when my first son was born, or the crazy day my second son was born and my first son ended up in hospital. It has helped me record the ups and downs of my life and cured me of that horrible High-FF habit of looking back and only seeing the bad stuff. I can honestly say that the years since starting my diary have been the best of my life – and I think writing a diary helped me not only remember that but realize it.

And if you think writing a diary embarrassing or cheesy or a bit angst ridden and prepubescent: fine. Get over it and write the diary anyway. If you stop reading this book now – never mind – but please start writing a diary. It is the single most transformative action you may ever take.

Case Study 4 – Dear diary

Two questions to the audience during my fear of failure evenings – who's done CBT and who keeps a diary? The two closely correlate, with many others (mostly female) saying they kept a diary at school but stopped after "growing up."

Asked why they kept a diary at school, the usual reasoning was that their diary "was like a friend" – helping them through those difficult years when alliances are formed and broken, and contradictory emotions run riot through their minds.

Yet in the days following one class, one of the adult diary-keepers wrote to me venturing a deeper reason for logging her daily thoughts.

"Since childhood I have suffered from manic depression," wrote Caroline, "and I find great comfort in writing my thoughts and feelings down in my diary. When writing, I find that it helps release some of the stress I feel, helping me cope with both that situation and the constant pain of my illness."

She described manic depression as a lonely illness, and her diary as a friend she can trust. Where she can express her emotions fully – ignoring concerns regarding inconsistencies, social positioning or the feelings of others.

"I never hold back my rage or sadness when writing in my diary," she wrote. "Like a friend, my diary is there for me in the good and bad moments – recording the joy and helping carry me through the agony."

It was the document that grounded her, she said – helping her realize that the bad days were followed by better days.

Caroline finished her email by saying she was now going to use it to guide her progress towards goal-achievement.

"I'd never considered using it this way, but it was obvious really," she wrote. "If all that ranting has a purpose – a goal – then it makes evaluation a whole lot easier. It is either useful or not useful, so immediately the emotions are being converted into thoughts I can use for my progress, which is marvellous."

What's Stopping You? *A major step towards negating the poor responses caused by neural hijackings is to use a diary to record and evaluate your thoughts. It will also be your map for plotting and recording your progress.*

PART TWO
Goals

PART TWO

<table>
<tr><td>5</td></tr>
<tr><td>ACT</td></tr>
</table>

In Part One I wrote that the most important line in Stephen Covey's *Seven Habits of Highly Effective People* involves our responses to external events, and the fact those responses are more important than the event itself. Well another line runs it a close second:

"Act or be acted upon."

He goes on to say that "the difference between people who exercise initiative and those who don't is literally the difference between night and day."

This is another of those universal recommendations across the self-help cosmos. Without proactivity we are lost, they all seem to agree. And, as with taking responsibility, this is at once a depressing but also liberating statement. A key factor in making progress involves our own actions – not those of somebody who may or may not like us, or may or may not take pity on us, or may or may not have our best interests at heart.

We no longer have to wait for that knight in shining armour. We *are* that knight in shining armour. To be able to act ourselves means that we are no longer acted upon. We are no longer someone else's tool, enslaved to their actions. It is *our* actions that matter, not those of a higher being or "saviour," or parent, teacher, boss or friend. And once we act we are expressing ourselves as an adult, potentially for the first time.

To be proactive is therefore a giant leap towards achievement motivation. Yet Covey warns us that proactive thinking is very different from positive thinking. By being proactive we are assessing things as they stand, which may be at their most negative. There is no gloss. It is what it is. Nonetheless, we are also stating that we can, and that we are willing, to do something about it.

Circle of influence

But do something about what? In order to be effective we need boundaries for our proactivity. And, luckily, Covey offers them – via a major point of mental differentiation. Any transformation to a more productive place requires the correct focus for our energies, which Covey maps by describing all external inputs into our life as being part of our Circle of Concern. However, some of these inputs are beyond our control, such as the weather, the traffic, or the actions of governments or large corporations.

What we can influence within the Circle of Concern – such as our own well-being and our work and home life – he calls our Circle of Influence. Obviously, this is a smaller circle, although it is the area that should be the focus of our every action. Anybody trying to take action to make progress in their life should concern themselves only with what they *can* change – their Circle of Influence – leaving areas where we have no influence both physically and mentally alone.

It is the world of the reactive person, Covey states, to spend their lives feeling angry and powerless (and even victimized) by what they perceive as the forces lined up against them, which – of course – they are helpless to do anything about. Proactive people, meanwhile, change what is changeable by focusing only on what is within their Circle of Influence.

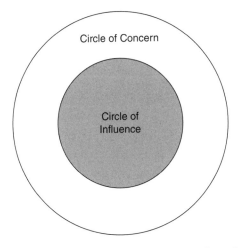

Figure 5.1 Focus on your circle of influence. Stephen Covey's circles of concern and influence.

Goals are a major differentiator

Having calculated that action is required and reconciled ourselves to the zone where action is possible we now need to direct that action. Any step is only a step forward if it is a step in the right direction. And that requires a plan. Without plans with discernable objectives we are directionless, and directionless people are either stuck in the same place or condemned to going round in circles.

"Without goals you simply drift and flow on the currents of life," wrote sales motivator Brian Tracy in his best-selling book *Goals!* (2003). "With goals, you fly like an arrow straight and true to your target."

Tracy describes life without goals as being similar to driving in thick fog. No matter how powerful the car we drive slowly and hesitantly, making little progress. Clear goals, meanwhile, enable us to "step on the accelerator."

Goals, therefore, make a big difference to both those that set them, and those that don't.

Yet for High-FFs, our fate can be worse than simply watching the goal-setters progress while we get left behind. Fearing failure with respect to our own ambitions (which we may have avoided setting, such is our fear), we are often recruited to help execute *their* plans, sometimes under the false premise that their goals are also our own (very much my own experience when starting Metrocube – see Part Five).

Indeed, in the absence of our own plan, we may as well adopt their goals. Those with a plan inspire confidence in others so, if we are directionless, we are bound to follow them. How can we make a decision if we don't know where we are going? How can we lead even ourselves? Decisions and leadership are for those that have direction, so directionless people often end up feeling they are best-off outsourcing their ambitions – even their decision-making – to someone who appears more able, simply because they have defined goals and therefore a clear path ahead of them.

According to Steve Chandler in *100 Ways to Motivate Yourself* (2001) in "life today, you are either living your dream of living someone else's. And unless you give your own dream the time and space it needs . . . you'll simply help others make their dreams come true."

Yet many High-FFs perceive themselves to be frustrated by others – usually those with high achievement motivation who seem to block our way while the path for them appears open. The difference between them and us, however, is often no more than the fact they are pursuing a detailed and preconceived plan and we are simply being dragged along by seemingly greater but invisible forces.

The grey zone

Goals also prevent us from entering what neuro-linguistic programming practitioner Lindsey Agness calls in *Change Your Life with NLP* (1998) the "grey zone" (more on NLP in chapter 6). This is where most High-FFs spend their lives: not destitute, quite comfortable even, but stuck and tremendously frustrated. It is a settlement for second best that will eat away at your happiness daily unless you enter what she calls the "awful zone" where things become so bad action becomes essential.

I can remember almost wishing for the awful zone to come – some disastrous moment that cleared the slate and allowed me to start again. I used to call it my "virtual suicide." With nothing to lose, I would surely lose my fear, I thought. Yet that day never arrived because I never made it happen. Instead I remained trapped in avoidance activities – simply "making a living" rather than designing a rewarding and fulfilling life. Goals, of course, would have circumnavigated the need for a "virtual suicide." Goals would have allowed me to see and plot a path upwards without having to hit rock-bottom first.

This leads on to what is perhaps the most fantastic thing about goal setting. The fact that the journey itself generates such a sense of excitement that we experience something of the sensation of arrival from the moment we take that first step. This is obvious to all but those with a high fear of failure simply because we have always been terrified of that first step. Yet we experience the same feeling when travelling. Just knowing that the destination is the airport and, after that, some exotic land of adventure makes that familiar first-leg drive through our home town that much sweeter.

Brian Tracy agrees with this, writing in *Goals!* that: "Goal-setting is so powerful that the very act of *thinking* about your goals makes you happy even before you have taken the first step towards achieving them."

Given this, imagine how you will feel after just a few positive and reaffirming steps along the path.

Tracy states that strong goals will make "you feel internally motivated to get up and get going every morning because every step you are taking will be moving you in the direction of something that is important to you."

Avoiding avoidance goals

Goal setting also reverses the psyche in the most profound way possible.

Tracy again: "Successful people think about what they want and how to get it," he writes, "while unsuccessful and unhappy people think about what they don't want and talk about their problems and worries and who is to blame."

Anthony Robbins (1992) wrote that the human mind is always in pursuit of an objective (Aristotle backs this up, opining that humans are a "teleological" organism, which means we are always moving towards something). So if we are not pursuing positive goals, says Robbins, we are pursuing the goal of eliminating or avoiding pain. These are negative or avoidance goals but, for the High-FF, they are probably the only real goals we have ever set.

Robbins states that it is the unconscious fear of disappointment that stops many people from setting positive and appropriate goals. Some may previously have set positive goals and failed to achieve them – resulting in an overwhelming fear of inflicting further pain. And this has led us to abandon positive goal-setting in order to avoid any renewed expectations also being dashed.

Yet the answer is not to hide from the pursuit of goals. The answer is to set the right goals. And these take time to calculate.

Setting the right goals

So what *do* you want? As a High-FF you will need to have an acute awareness of the fact you may set inappropriate goals – at both extremes – for fear of Atkinson's High-FF peg-hooping avoidance tactics mentioned in Part One. You may yet aim too low or too high because you secretly view yourself as incapable of achieving even moderately challenging goals.

So how can you tell if you have the right goals – other than by waiting for potentially the wrong result? Not easy. For instance, at

Moorgate we often discuss with clients the need to look beneath the surface when it comes to setting objectives for our PR campaigns.

Properly brainstorming objectives can reveal that the real goals are not always the obvious ones. There have been times when we have set the wrong objectives, which has led to the wrong strategy and the wrong tactics (more on strategy and tactics in Part Three) – something that has sometimes only become apparent after achieving the wrong results.

For instance, we had one banking client whose stated objective was to win new clients. Yet he was determined to do this by profiling himself in the international financial press. He was unimpressed by trade or regional publications, he stated, and thought a profile in the *Financial Times* or *Wall Street Journal* the only way to get noticed.

Of course, we failed to win him the coverage he wanted as his messages were too specific. Yet when we dug further it turned out his real objective was to impress his bosses who were thinking of cutting funding for the department. This knowledge meant we could change the strategy and tactics accordingly – eventually creating a series of newsletters that detailed his deal successes and included interviews with happy clients. We then circulated them both internally (upstairs) and externally to new or potential clients. He was delighted with the results.

This is no less the case with our own lives. Just being busy and taking action is pointless unless we are pursuing the right goals, which are not always obvious. Covey writes about getting caught up in "busy-ness" or the "activity trap."

He describes a parable in which an exploratory group hack their way through a jungle only for their leader to climb the tallest tree, survey the landscape, and shout: "wrong jungle."

"Shut up," says the manager in the ground, "we are making progress."

If our ladder is not leaning against the right wall, he states, then every step up just takes us further from our real goals. We are heading to the wrong place faster.

So how do we find the right jungle to cut through or wall for our ladder? And how can we trust that we have set the right goals? This takes some intense visualization, some deep thinking and some soul-searching – all of which is to come.

Case Study 5 – Finding her own path

Fiona had a successful career as a qualified management accountant, something she'd pursued since university. Indeed, her diligence and aptitude meant she'd risen to the position of chief financial officer for two mid-sized companies – leading both to a successful sale to larger rivals.

Yet such a course had never felt anything more than what was expected of her. She'd pursued the goals of others, she thought. Now 39, and with the second sale complete (resulting in a payout), she was determined to find her own path.

"I wasn't unhappy," she said when we met for a coffee. "I've done good things. But they were never *my* things. My entire life, I feel that I've done what others have expected of me."

From our chat it emerged that her weakness was the strength and direction of others. Having been influenced by others in her academic and career choices, she now realized she'd outsourced her entire career path – following strong, ambitious personalities that possessed the direction she'd lacked.

Yet, having made her second entrepreneurial boss rich, she felt deflated. And her mild "is that all" funk had sharpened into a discontent at the direction she'd taken.

After reading *What's Stopping You?* Fiona started writing a daily diary to record her thoughts and feelings, and this led to the germ of an idea.

"I've never had a problem with motivation," said Fiona. "But the only time I was really engaged – for myself – was when working on problem-based projects during my mathematics degree at university. I thought applying maths in this way was fascinating and beautiful, not least because it took in such a broad range of subjects."

"I'm interested in the environment and want to teach environmental economics at university," she finally declared.

Reconciled to the five-year journey through post-graduate studies and PhDs, she felt a buzz of excitement about dedicating herself to her primary love, but as a teacher rather than a student.

What's Stopping You? *Without proactivity you are condemned to make no progress in your life. And without goals you are prone to becoming the tools of those with goals. Yet strong goal-setting can generate excitement and positivity before you have even taken the first step.*

6

VISUALIZATION

In the previous chapter I quoted from Lindsey Agness's book *Change Your Life With NLP*. Now seems like a good moment to discuss NLP or neuro-linguistic programming given that this section – on visualization of goals – owes more than a little to that happy band of self-motivators. Many modern self-help books are either openly or indirectly using NLP in their framework of actions. And millions of people with low self-esteem or low confidence have undoubtedly had their lives improved by adopting NLP techniques.

For those with a high fear of failure, however, some caution is required.

NLP emerged in the 1970s as a radically new approach to psychotherapy and personal change based on, according to the *Oxford English Dictionary* (2009), "a model of interpersonal communication chiefly concerned with the relationship between successful patterns of behaviour and the subjective experiences (esp. patterns of thought) underlying them."

The aim is that awareness of the way both we and others think, speak and behave – and changes in patterns of behaviour and speech based on this awareness – can help people achieve success. NLP has more than a casual link with CBT in this respect, although NLP is CBT on steroids – claiming that adopters can influence the reactions of others to achieve positive external results, rather than simply helping us re-evaluate our responses to external events.

Fine. Yet many NLP practitioners go way beyond understanding thoughts and actions, or even "modelling" the successful behaviour of others. Start researching the claims of the more extreme NLP practitioners and we soon discover offers for rapid and transformational change, with some claiming that wholesale changes can be made in our unconscious mind – including removal of our fears and phobias – almost instantly, even using techniques such as hypnotherapy (and self-hypnosis) in order to achieve this. And with our fears seemingly banished forever, some practitioners also claim that a furious and headlong drive towards "dream fulfilment" is possible.

Of course, such strong claims make NLP both an alluring and potentially dangerous tool in the hands of High-FFs prone to seeking instant change, or to thinking that they can be rewired, or to pursuing inappropriate avoidance-based goals.

NLP needs tempering

While gratefully acknowledging NLP ideas and methodology, therefore, we must remain acutely aware that the stated outcomes from NLP-rooted exercises, including visualization, may need to be tempered. NLP's critics state that established neuroscience does not support claims regarding the potential for rewiring our self-beliefs, including our fears, meaning that NLP may offer no more than a deeper form of self-denial or perhaps tenuous and refutable "success" through the power of suggestion.

And while I'm not taking sides with respect to NLP's veracity, it is my belief that the moment of realization regarding our faulty wiring, false evaluations and destructive self-belief, is an important one for those with fear of failure. It needs to be examined and understood – nurtured even. Not swapped for a headlong pursuit in the other direction.

There is no transformational technique that can make that monkey disappear. And any attempt at distancing ourselves from him could see him painfully snap back like over-stretched elastic. As High-FFs, we are hardwired to our primary beliefs and default settings, no matter how faulty. They are coming with us, I am afraid, and – in my view – sustainable, long-term progress towards achievement motivation is only possible once we realize this and accept it.

Of course, many people who have thought themselves drowning in a sea of insecurities have found strength, purpose and buoyancy through NLP – and that's great (sincerely meant). Yet as a lifeboat, NLP can perhaps be compared to *Alcoholics Anonymous*, with the "recovering" alcoholics having the upper hand in one key respect. They have to reaffirm their addiction at every meeting, meaning they are not permitted any form of self-denial. So while an alcoholic has to introduce themselves with the affirmation "my name's [Janet] and I'm an alcoholic," some of those I meet using NLP seem to offer the more proselytizing: "my name's [John], and *you* are the insecure one."

This is an important point for those with fear of failure to grasp in my opinion. We are "recovering" High-FFs – trying to overcome our insecurities and fears just as alcoholics are trying to overcome their addiction. There is no final victory, just a more promising path and the avoidance of destructive thoughts or behaviour.

There's a wider point here about anyone using *any* form of self-help to improve their lives. Strong short-term progress can lead us into becoming preaching motivational converts – not only seeing insecurities in everyone we meet but offering unsolicited advice. No matter what resources we use for self-improvement, we must remember that it is only *our* behaviour that we are seeking to change, not those of our friends or acquaintances – and especially not those of strangers we feel are in need of enlightenment.

Visualization of goals

The above warning on the limits of NLP for High-FFs seeking "recovery" from their fear of failure is necessary simply because of what happens next – the visualization of our goals as so excellently recommended by many of the more professional and enlightened NLP practitioners.

Famous hotelier Conrad Hilton kept a photo of New York's Waldorf Hotel under the glass on his desk. It remained there for 18 years until he bought the hotel. The photo was a daily visual reminder of his goal, giving him the focus he needed to achieve it.

"We are what we are because we have first imagined it," writes Anthony Robbins (1992), adding that setting goals through visualization is the first step in turning the invisible (our future) into the visible.

It certainly worked for me. In my early days as an entrepreneur I organized and attended a seminar at *Metrocube*, held by one of the UK's leading NLP practitioners. At the seminar she did a curious thing – making us all close our eyes and imagine ourselves 10 years hence.

For instance, how were we dressed? This is important as it starts giving an indication about us as people. We were asked to visualize our perfect selves so the assumption was we were dressed well, but in what: summer casuals, a Savile Row suit, the Barbour and wellies of a country squire, or in something from a Paris or Milan catwalk? And who had we become as people? For instance, what is our place of work like? Is it an office in Mayfair, a farmhouse kitchen table, something sleek in a Manhattan skyscraper, or even a workshop under the Brighton railway?

Is it our own company, or are we high up in our target organization (or even just doing the right job in our target organization)? Indeed, can we identify our target organization, as well as the right job?

And who works for us? Is there a team, a partner, a PA, a receptionist, a hierarchy of people below us, or the perfect line manager above? What do they look like? What are *they* wearing in the office?

Perhaps the most important aspect is our home life. Where is our house: Maida Vale, California, the Cotswolds, Provence,

Sydney? What does it look like? Is it old or new, four stories or a bungalow, peg-tiled or flat-roofed? Does it have a gravel drive or is it a Belgravia mansion on to a square? Is it our only house or are there others? What does it look like inside: the hall, the kitchen, the study, the bedrooms, the bathroom? What is it like outside: acres of lawn and mature trees, a formal garden, a balcony with a cool cityscape view, or maybe a ramshackle farmyard?

And who are we with? Is it our current partner or someone new? Are there kids? If so how many? What are their names? Dogs, horses, snakes, fish? What are *their* names?

One thing I remember is just how much detail our NLP practitioner sought. We were actually projecting ourselves into our bedroom or office, actually greeting our colleagues and partners, actually stroking the dog and wandering the grounds of our house.

Parcelling up the 10-year goals

There are several versions of visualization. Another imagines speakers at our funeral, although I like the 10-year version (Anthony Robbins also has a 10-year horizon) because it contains lots of detail and – crucially – it allows us to parcel-up the expanse of time in front of us. The 10-year visualization exercise gives us a whole decade to reach our goals. That house, office, career and dog does not have to be in place until the end of year nine, month 11, day 30.

However, you do need to take the right steps towards it today. After your 10-year visualization, therefore, an important next task is to visualize where you would have to be in five years to make that 10-year goal achievable. Again, details please – what does every aspect look and feel like? Then what about in two years' time – where would you have to be in 24 months to meet those five year goals? Again, lots and lots of detail. And what about in 12 months? Where would you have to be to meet the two-year goal? The same goes for six months, then one month then one week. It is obvious where this ends up. What has to happen tomorrow to meet the one week goal, and what can be done *now* in preparation for tomorrow's actions?

Lurid fantasies

Yet there's an important caveat to this process. For any "recovering" High-FF aiming to adopt the behaviours of those with high achievement motivation alarm bells should have been ringing during the 10-year visualization exercise as we may have indulged ourselves in the most lurid fantasies imaginable. We are encouraged to "play a role," which means many of us could well have lost ourselves opting for the Beverley Hills mansion with its own recording studio, a guitar-shaped swimming pool and lots of gorgeous and sexually available people hanging on to our every word.

Despite what many self-motivators will say such fantasies could well be inappropriate goals, not because it is out of reach but because, as High-FFs, we chose it simply because it was, indeed, out of reach. There was no, or little, emotional cost in fantasizing at this level because we knew it was never going to happen – at least short of a major lottery win (see below on the lottery). Such indulgences may well be counterproductive for the recovering High-FF as these are hardly the challenging but achievable and rewarding goals of those with achievement motivation. This, to me, looks like a potentially dangerous encouragement to throw the hoop towards the peg from as far back as possible.

Picking the right jungle

It is worth noting here that this book is not saying "get real" and perhaps end up with a small promotion and one extra bedroom. It is a book aimed at helping those with a high fear of failure to understand what has happened to them and how they can use this knowledge to calculate better responses that help them achieve better results in the future.

If it leads us permanently away from the High-FF prison of negative self-fulfilling responses to the sunlit uplands of achievement motivation then that is a massive, *massive*, success – and one that cannot be measured in guitar-shaped swimming pools. And goal-setting is a vital part of this – *the* most vital part, in fact, as it is about pointing us in the right direction after having spent a lifetime stuck in the wrong place and facing the wrong way thanks to the purgatory of our fears and insecurities.

The most vital action you can take at this point, therefore, is to generate goals that matter to *you*. Goals that are yours – not the fantasies fed to you by marketing men exploiting your vulnerabilities, or by Simon Cowell, Anthony Robbins or any other star maker or guru. Only then will the goals be sustainable and achievable. Only then will you, slowly – over many years – prevent your fear of failure from derailing your progress as you, step-by-step, move towards your goals.

The Character Ethic

Stephen Covey of *Seven Habits* . . . fame is probably the high priest of appropriate goal setting, although his true genius for those with a high fear of failure is that he doesn't ask us to reinvent ourselves or deny our past pain in order to make progress: quite the opposite. He argues against what he calls the "Personality Ethic" prevalent in most modern self-help books and instead promotes the "Character Ethic."

The Personality Ethic, states Covey, relies on developing skills and techniques that can result in quick success. However, these may be revealed as insincere (even manipulative) and will lose their lustre as soon as we hit a major difficulty that the techniques cannot deal with. The Personality Ethic forces us to wear a mask – to display a personality that is inconsistent with our character. Such masks could include the confident, witty or attractive person that the self-help books and techniques are trying to promote – stating that this person is within us and waiting to come out, when in fact we are being asked to express ourselves based on learnt or acquired behaviours that are the opposite to our inner selves.

The Character Ethic, meanwhile, is based on developing a character that complements our principles – in fact is "principles-centred." This is a long-term process aimed at bearing fruit according to natural law, i.e. over years (Covey uses a farming analogy of things taking time to propagate and grow). There are *no* short cuts or quick-fixes.

And from our principles-centred character all goals and behaviours flow. We need to develop and explore the principles that provide the blank canvass upon which we draw our map. Covey's call is that we formulate goals based on principles that he claims are innate in human beings: including fairness, integrity, honesty, human dignity, quality and excellence. They also include the idea of human potential, growth and encouragement.

The principles come first

My first reading of this made me hesitate, I have to admit. I was absorbed in a book focused on making me more effective and was instead getting a lecture on ethics and morality. It felt too holy for me, too sanctimonious – dare I say it: too American. Many of the most effective people I have ever met were scoundrels – immorally and unethically pursuing their self-interest with no care for the external consequences (a lack of concern that I secretly admired, so wrapped up was I in what other people thought of me). Certainly, they were not "principles-centred." In fact, many were so eaten up with ambition they were deeply unprincipled, although I recognize now that this may have been due to their inner frustrations and insecurities.

But then the penny dropped. I wasn't trying to become one of these people, however much I secretly envied them. I was trying to move away from High-FF behaviour (which many of them displayed) and towards high achievement motivation. I was prepared to accept there were no short cuts to doing this. And having to accept that this involved setting goals that were principles-centred was just another step, which I eventually took.

I realized Covey is right. When I studied myself in depth I didn't find a bad person despite some shamefully spiteful and selfish acts. I found a good person with a burning sense of injustice about how the world had treated me thus far. Those very moments of bad behaviour were based on feelings of frustration, which I had always inwardly justified as such – to the point of feeling shocked and harshly judged when my behaviour had been pulled up by others.

In fact I had often mused that inside every bad person was a good person trying to get out. Many muggers, bank robbers, even murderers would inwardly justify their actions based on prejudice against them or poor opportunities. Most would see themselves as, at heart, a good person. Certainly, frustration has been a key driver for my bad behaviour over the years. Remove the frustration, I reasoned, and the principles-centred good guy would come forth.

And Covey was simply saying I had this the wrong way round. Being principles-centred means that the hidden good person within needs to come to the fore *first* in order to act as a benchmark and driver for our new goals and behaviours. We must move towards the person we want to be – emotionally and spiritually – not become that person only once we have arrived at some new destination. In terms of principles, the journey and the destination are one and the same. And they start here.

This was one of those revelatory moments for me. It confirmed two things: that my internal fight between the good and bad me is a crucial battle in my quest to overcome my fear of failure, and that the good person is innate – I had simply developed bad thoughts and behaviours from bad experiences. It also confirmed that the future would be better than the past because I now realized this and could act accordingly – using my principles to act as a strong benchmark for my goal setting, as well as my future behaviour.

I then had another revelation, about the unprincipled people I'd envied. In my careers there had been a few but, looking back, I realized that none of these people had prospered. One had lost his job after arrogantly conducting an affair in the office, another had run his company into the ground after playing fast and loose with his creditors, and then there were my colleagues who found themselves in prison after pleading guilty to fraud-related charges. Just maybe being principles-centred was also the most sustainable way to proceed.

Our own constitution

Having encouraged a principles-centred orientation Covey then states we must use that centre to generate appropriate, long-term and enduring goals. But we first have to write a personal mission statement that includes our values and principles.

Covey invoked the example of the *US Constitution* – a document I studied at university and had admired for its brevity, accuracy and totemic qualities. The *US Constitution* (along with the *Bill of Rights* included within it) encapsulated the principles and values of the new republic and set a very clear standard for future generations to adhere to. Covey wrote that the *US Constitution* made it crystal clear when such standards had been breached: during the Watergate scandal for instance. And such is the grounding of that document that it is my belief that it was an important building block in the creation of the US as a superpower.

So there are clear advantages for creating your own constitution. It is not a document that should be scribbled or hurried, however. Think about it over days and weeks, and add to it over a period of time. Anthony Robbins talks of writing our goals rapidly without pause, which is fine for a first draft. However, *Your Constitution* is something that needs to be honed. You should also consider it the first "action" in your recovery from fear of failure and then commit it to your diary (perhaps in those back pages marked "notes"), which will give you the opportunity to review it annually.

My Constitution (for illustrative purposes only – in my view this is a deeply private document):

- To be a strong mentor and example to my children.
- To give my children confidence and self-esteem.
- To honour my marriage vows – that's why I made them.
- To create a career I am proud of.
- To create a legacy from the work I do.
- To seek happiness but to accept that happiness comes from within.
- To recognize failings and mistakes and to make amends.
- To recognize that my irritation and impatience with others is not their failing but mine.
- To act with integrity and to honour my debts.
- To not work purely for money.
- To realize that my first reaction is not always the correct one.
- To "never surrender."

Given the above, it is hard to see how being a hotshot investment banker or humorous laddish writer were ever appropriate goals for me to pursue.

And there is an important point here about ambitions. If you genuinely think a key element of *Your Constitution* is "to be rich" or "to be famous" then you should include it. But it may also be worth asking yourself "why?" If the deep and genuine answer is "because I want to drive a Ferrari" or "because I want to be recognized in the street" that's fine. But what if the deep and genuine answer is "to show everyone that I am not worthless?" Then a better line for *Your Constitution* may be "to prove my worth," with more specific objectives consigned to the 10-year visualization. Remember, *Your Constitution* is about developing your principles.

It's not about your dream job or what brand of jeans you want to wear in five years' time.

A dynamic towards appropriate goal setting

Your Constitution is aimed at getting you to the next stage: developing specific objectives and milestones – as defined by our principles. Others agree with Covey on this. According to Brian Tracy (2003), our values define us – generating the following dynamic towards appropriate goal setting:

(a)   First we discover our values,
(b)   We then determine our beliefs from our values,
(c)   We derive our attitude from our beliefs,
(d)   We arrive at our expectations from our attitudes, and, finally,
(e)   We set our actions from our expectations.

If we reverse this chain it is easy to see where things go wrong for the High-FF. Our expectations of failure mean that we set inappropriate goals because of our beliefs that we are incapable of achievement. This incapacity is derived from our values, which include placing a higher focus on maintaining face than on achievement.

But just say we were to start with more appropriate, principle-based, values and then run these through Tracy's dynamic. If a core value was to focus on continual self-improvement, our beliefs must be that continuous self-improvement is possible, which will surely have a beneficial impact on our attitude towards learning – it is there to help us live by our core values. This attitude fuels positive expectations regarding self-improvement and drives our actions.

Suddenly, we are facing the right way with some clear values and principles to achieve and maintain. Project these forward and we can indulge ourselves in those NLP visualizations to help us define our goals in detail.

Goal-setting may take several goes

And if, by the end of all these exercises, you do not have a well thought through and achievable action plan for the next 10 years, then you need to go back to *Your Constitution* and think again about your principles and values. This is nothing to beat yourself up about. It may take several goes. And realizing that the goals need resetting at this stage is a lot less painful than realizing this five years down the line (although be aware that goals may, can and should change).

Your actions now are based on putting the ladder against the right wall so answers may not be instant. The visualization may take a few goes, as may *Your Constitution*. That's fine. You have a lifetime to get this right (with the first 10 years our immediate focus) and the journey is likely to be a lot nicer than the painful and bumpy ride you have so far experienced.

Case Study 6 – Changing values

Being a mum had changed Louise. And this had confused her true values, which triggered her email to me. Over coffee she told me of her strong pre-parenting career in advertising, working for one of London's top agencies. Yet she also told me of her five-year career gap, which had left her wondering about her place within this competitive and fashion-conscious profession.

"With my second child now entering school I was running out of excuses not to return to work," she said. "But my confidence was low because of such a long gap. I started by taking on part-time project work from my old agency but I hated the fact that my male contemporaries were now my seniors, which meant I had to work with the juniors who were all, well, so young and *so* ambitious."

"I had none of their drive," she confessed. "And I could tell they thought me a lightweight – someone just serving time for a salary."

"The juniors were a tight group, as I remember we were when I was starting," she said. "And I can also remember what we thought of the older part-time mums. They were out of ideas and not very interested in the job, we thought. Distracted by baby."

"And here I was proving myself right with my own self-fulfilling behaviour," said Louise.

"It didn't help that I couldn't work late or go to the social functions," she said. "But nor did I want to. I had other priorities, and the evening brainstorming sessions followed by drinks in the pub or some event bored me."

In fact even Louise's view of advertising had changed.

"Where once there was passion, there was now contempt," she said. "At the cocky 20-somethings, at the vain seniors, at the self-regarding campaigns. I guess I'd fallen deeply out of love with advertising, but I needed to work so I had no choice but to put up with it."

Her two daughters were now her core focus, she said, after I asked her about her true values. It was *their* needs, *their* future, *their* education that mattered to Louise.

And, of course, her indifference began to impact her work. She was soon in the senior's office (a former contemporary) discussing her problems with relating to the young team now directing her work.

That did it for Louise, although it was also what prompted her question to me.

"How can *Your Constitution* be carved in stone," she asked, "when it is so obvious my values have utterly changed. Wouldn't that have set me along the wrong path?"

I was keen to explain that, far from carved in stone, we renew *our constitution* annually, or at least check it as we transfer the bullet points from one diary to the next. So it's a fluid document (as is the *US Constitution*, which has 26 amendments). It's there to act as our guiding light when visualizing our goals, I said.

"Having to pursue an objective based on a true value you no longer hold is dispiriting," I agreed. "Yet the annual renewal should allow for the gentle evolution of our values – perhaps to reflect our life-cycle while hopefully avoiding the lurching changes that may themselves be reversed after further reflections or poor experiences."

Louise left to pick up her children – offering the parting shot that she was looking into becoming a primary school teacher. I was delighted for her but offered the caveat that her new values may also change as her children grow up.

"Don't worry – I'm aware of that," she said, and hurried off.

What's Stopping You? *Visualizing your desired destination 10 years hence is a strong starting point for goal-setting – especially when divided into milestones that connect now with then. But avoiding inappropriate goal-setting requires you first to develop Your Constitution based on your principles and values, although be aware that your values may evolve as you progress.*

7

LANGUAGE AND BEHAVIOUR

The point of all this goal-setting activity is, of course, to generate proactivity. And a key element of proactive behaviour is proactive language.

"The right words can have a galvanizing effect, generating enthusiasm, energy, momentum and more, while the wrong words can undermine the best intentions and kill initiative on the spot, stone dead," writes leadership guru Stephen Denning in *The Secret Language of Leadership* (2007).

Whether it is *Your Constitution*, your goal-setting, your diary, or simply your thoughts and speech, you need to adopt the right tone and vocabulary.

Covey (1989) points out that reactive language is based on absolving us – "that's just the way I am," "there's nothing I can do" and so on. It is saying "I'm not responsible," "I was born this way."

But you *are* responsible. You were not born this way. You became this way through your own responses and behaviours, whatever the external root causes. In fact you became this way partly because of the language you used. Reactive or defeatist language is – like fear itself – self-fulfilling.

Write down your goals

Luckily we have a major opportunity to put this right. Having been through the goal-setting visualization exercises you now need to write them down. And while writing them down is an opportunity to re-evaluate your goals and ensure they make sense – that the one year is connected to the two-year and so on up to the 10-year summit – they are also an opportunity to adopt the right tone and language.

This is not rocket science. For instance, you should write the goals in present-tense language. Lindsey Agness (2008) states that we should behave as if we are already there – that our goals have already been achieved – which also holds true for the language we use when writing our goals. For instance, if we make the journey as certain as a train ride we are compelled to take the steps that propel us forward.

"We arrive at Manchester Piccadilly Station at 16:45," says the announcer on the *Virgin* train.

"Year 10: we are living in a self-built six-bedroom house in Norfolk with three horses, two dogs and a rare breed of sheep."

Are we? *Wow* – have we named all the sheep yet?

Goals need to be that specific, involving – according to Julie Starr, MD of Starr Counselling in *The Coaching Manual* (2002) – the what, where, when and whom.

"I want more energy," is too vague, she states, and therefore less motivating than "I want more energy to be able to play sports with my kids after work."

Add the timescale (each week), venue (at the new leisure centre) and the sport (badminton) and the objective is just one phone call and a quick trip to a sports shop (probably located within the leisure centre) from being converted into sustainable action.

Behave as if we are already there

The process of "behaving as if you are already there" and using language that supports this contention is an important one because it produces new more positive neural pathways in the brain. And these are built upon with each positive step in the right direction.

We cannot aim at achievement motivation and continue to behave in ways dictated by our fear of failure. If necessary, we have to "fake it til we make it" to use the expression of many self-help writers, most notably Tom Bay and David Macpherson in *Change Your Attitude* (1998).

If you want to be promoted, they suggest, you have to act as if you already have been – taking on the airs of the seniors, adopting their seriousness and dropping the office clown persona that may have been a mask for your disappointments. Over time this will become an unconscious habit and will become noticed by those in the hierarchy above you.

Obviously there may be limits to this. The Norfolk farm in year-10 is a strong goal but turning up to work in our green wellies may raise a few eyebrows. Spending the weekend in wellies scouring Norfolk for the perfect location, on the other hand, is fine – especially if, like Conrad Hilton, we then keep a photo of it on our desk.

Having said this, your goal-centred behaviours are necessarily different from your behaviours as a High-FF. You may find that the behavioural traits that chained you to the floor (such as clowning) are the very traits that made you popular with particular people (often fellow High-FFs). These traits have to change, for sure – but there is no need to change your friends. You could instead add to *Your Constitution* "to radiate positivity."

Positive self-talk

Negative self-talk also has to go, to be replaced with positive self-talk.

According to John Caunt (2003) you should cut yourselves some slack – questioning negative thoughts and opinions and recognizing instead your positive qualities, even writing down (in the usual place) strong statements of support that help recast your set beliefs and reframe your outlook using "half full" rather than "half empty" language.

In *Change Your Attitude*, Bay and Macpherson implore us to overcome the negative self-talk, stating that everyone has inbuilt negative self-talk tapes they need to destroy. Instead, we should learn to compliment ourselves, they state, which is true at every level – even if you are simply recording those small but accumulating achievements in your diary.

And goals should be stated in positive terms, moving towards what you want rather than avoiding what you don't want. Aims such as "I don't want to be poor" are meaningless, they state, and should be replaced with positive and more specific statements such as "I want to be able to afford the four bedroom house in that leafy neighbourhood I've always coveted." Explore why you want *that* house, and you're probably getting closer still to a more constitutional assessment of what really motivates you.

Yet all this positive talk must not lead you into a false paradigm. The words used have to be authentically yours or you will be fooling yourself. How can you tell? Not easy, especially in the early days when our "natural state" seems to come with such a negative dialogue. Injecting positive language into such a pessimistic outlook feels like walking back into a stadium as the fans pour out after the final whistle.

Wait a little longer, however, and the crowds are gone. Go back into the stadium and you can shout what you like and it will echo off the rafters. And by writing down your goals you are giving yourself that space to turn around your thinking, as well as change your language from negative to positive. You are deliberately no longer part of the crowd and you can adopt what language you like.

However, positive next steps that are written and then ignored perhaps need to be examined. Is there a reason you have not enrolled onto that language or accountancy course? Maybe your desire to learn Japanese or qualify as an accountant is something that has been fed to you from elsewhere. Maybe it was never *your* goal in the first place, and an art foundation course or small business enterprise scheme would be far more motivating.

Pre- and post-visualization exercises

Goal-setting is harder work than it first appears and requires time and soul searching, although there are many pre-visualization exercises you can try if you are struggling to set appropriate goals.

One comes from Jim Cairo in *Motivation and Goal Setting* (1998), who states that the importance of setting goals that are consistent with your true identity is vital as these goals will sustain your motivation over time. And if you are struggling with determining your true self (a common problem for those with fear of failure) Cairo suggests ranking the following attributes 1-to-10 in importance:

- Security
- Wealth
- Good health
- Relationship with partner
- Relationship with kids
- Relationship with family
- Fame
- Job/career
- Power
- Happiness
- Friendship
- Retirement
- Owning your own business
- Long life
- Travel
- Respect of peers
- Spiritual fulfilment
- Charity

What are the highest-ranking attributes? These should get 80 per cent of your time and form a basis for your goal setting, says

Cairo. And they can feed into *Your Constitution*, which remains your key grounding document for goal-setting.

And there are post goal-setting exercises we can employ to ensure we are on the right path. Lindsey Agness (2008) quotes well-known success guru Paul J. Meyer who recommends the mnemonic SMART when assessing our goal-setting.

According to Meyer, our objectives should be:

- Specific (not "lose weight" but "lose 10 pounds")
- Measurable ("lose 10 pounds by June")
- Achievable (i.e. within the bounds of possibility – travel to Mars, for instance, may be a few generations hence)
- Realistic (maybe a half marathon is more realistic this year, with a full marathon next year)
- Timed ("June" it is)

Yet care is needed with measurable objectives – especially those that are time-related. If your aim is to be CEO within a year, changing course on day 365 may be self-defeating. As Anthony Robbins states, many people give up their goals having passed a time-related deadline without realizing they were within days of achieving their objective. Certainly, being too strict with time horizons can be self-defeating.

The Reticular Activating System – our "antennae"

What is not necessary at this stage is any consideration regarding *how* our goals will be achieved. Mike Dooley "dream fulfilment" guru and author of *Notes from the Universe* (2007), calls these the "dreaded hows." His view is that there are a million ways to achieve something, so it is crazy to establish now the how for a goal three years hence. Only for the next milestone should there be any consideration for the "how."

The secret to "manifesting change," he states, is not focusing on the how but on the desired end result. This seems to chime with just about everybody else I've read on this, although a key additional point he makes is that once we are truly focused on our desired end result "the universe will conspire on our behalf."

In fact, it's not the universe that conspires in our favour once we have cleared the path in front of us to focus on our goals: it is us. Our Reticular Activating System (RAS) does the work. This is the area of the brain responsible for regulating arousal and is composed of several neuronal circuits connecting the brainstem to the cortex.

No, this didn't mean much to me either – at least not until I realized the RAS is what I used to call "my antennae" – the element of my consciousness that seems to notice things I am currently focused on. For instance, I was given a Burberry scarf for Christmas. It was lovely, and I have worn it every day so far this winter. Yet since Christmas I have noticed these scarves everywhere on the streets of London – on professionals walking to work, students going to college, day-trippers in Oxford Street.

Why had I not noticed these scarves before? Because my RAS was only alerted to them on Christmas Day when I opened my mother's gift. Only since then has it bothered to draw my attention to just how many of these scarves are out there. Previously my brain had filtered out the scarves, like 99.9 per cent of the information it receives, because it meant nothing to me.

Yet for those with a high fear of failure, our RAS has picked up mostly negative stimuli until now. For instance, if we assume there is prejudice against us, the RAS seeks it out (and inevitably finds it). If, however, we focus on our goals – especially ones with the next steps laid out in front of us – anything relevant that passes our senses, sticks. And that's a lot of information. I've often heard people be amazed at the right solution or the right person or the right idea appearing as if from nowhere at exactly the right moment. Yet they hadn't appeared from nowhere. Our RAS found them when they had previously gone unnoticed.

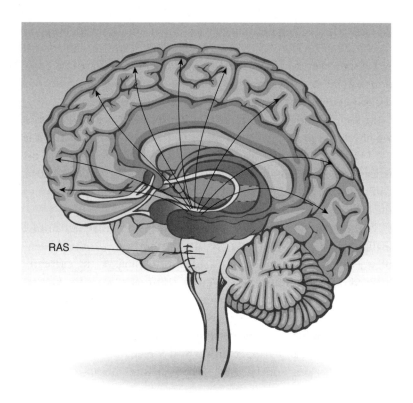

Figure 7.1 The Reticular Activating System

Luck and the winner's curse

One last point on this. The more I read about our RAS the more it occurs to me that it may also have an impact on luck – that key ingredient that those with high achievement motivation seem to have in abundance and us High-FFs seem to lack. Certainly, I have always considered myself unlucky – to the point where I would joke about the "Kelsey Effect" on any company, car, girlfriend, house, street, city or country I alighted upon. Bad things would immediately and unexpectedly start happening to them. And my wife likes to joke about the "Kelsey Cloud" that always seems to follow us on our summer holidays (we even had rain on our trip to the Sahara Desert!).

Yet I noticed that my "luck" seemed to change when I became focused on a particular goal, at least with respect to that goal. Opportunities would appear at the right moment and obstacles disappear. And this I now realize was not luck at all: it was my RAS.

There are also positives to feeling unlucky. I have always hated gambling because of my poor "luck," but now consider this a blessing. To me, gambling is the "winner's curse" – the arrogance of the "lucky" making them over-estimate purely mathematical probabilities. More-often-than-not gambling results in the most rapid levelling of the "lucky" and the "unlucky" known to man. Thank heavens – and my own High-FF status – that I've avoided that fate.

This extends even to the lottery, which I have never "played" and would beg any recovering High-FF to avoid. Not only is it a "tax on the stupid" as one clever friend described it, the lottery offers an excuse for inaction when there is no excuse for inaction.

"When I win the lottery," makes me cringe every time I hear it.

It's not the lottery that will change your life. It's you.

Assuming poor luck has also led me towards a hatred of "winging it" in meetings and presentations. I am consistently the best briefed and prepped, precisely because I assumed I had to make amends for my poor luck.

Certainly, I have assumed the odds were stacked against me in just about any walk of life, which has, over the years, led to things working out more and more in my favour. As a young person the cocky assurance of those with high achievement motivation is an obvious advantage when it comes to winning the girl/boy or convincing employers to give them that first break. But life is a marathon, not a sprint, and luck will inevitably go against those relying on that most ephemeral of qualities. Meanwhile, I assumed poor luck from the start, which has prepared me well for the inevitable puddles – many of which I can now deftly sidestep.

Case Study 7 – The ambition of no ambition

Andrew was an old friend from home. A nice guy, he was never in fights – roguish but no rebel, thus winning the approval of both his peers and the grown-ups. He was also bright, with a strong future ahead of him: until tragedy struck. A motorbike accident left him with a broken leg and Debra, the love of his life as well as his passenger, dead.

His future changed. He lost interest in formalized career paths, instead becoming something of a dropout. I caught up with him 10 years later, busking on a San Francisco corner. He recognized me and called my name, but it took me a moment to recognize him so radically had he changed: tattoos, piercings, braided hair and clothes that would these days euphemistically be described as "festival-going."

We went for a drink and he described his route to that corner – mostly involving travel, busking, and more travel. He'd been everywhere: going from hostel to hostel and bonding with the gap-year kids 10 years his junior.

He was happy, and still a nice guy, but he knew he'd come off the rails.

"Sure the accident changed my life," he said. "But it also made me think about what mattered, and what didn't."

He'd adopted the language and mannerisms of the itinerate lifestyler, which became more exaggerated as the evening wore on and he described the beauty of his life "on the open road."

"The places I see, the people I meet, the songs I write – they're a lot more beautiful than the life of some pen-pusher back home," he said.

I left him talking to two girls. They were planning their trip and he was keen to hitch a ride in their camper van, although he was obviously "totally laid back" about the idea of it "not being cool."

Looking back, I can now see that Andrew had developed a persona aimed at dealing with his pain. His ambition had been to have no ambition, perhaps because he inwardly felt he deserved no future. Yet something about his happiness made me sad for him, although it was probably no more than part of his grieving process. And who was I to judge, even at this distance?

Years later, Andrew reconnected via a social-media website. Back in the UK, he'd married and prospered and was focused on the future. Meanwhile, those tattoos have become the height of fashion.

What's Stopping You? *Positive language is important when goal-setting, as is "behaving as if you are already there." Yet while your goals have to be detailed, you should avoid focusing on the "dreaded hows" – not least because your RAS will help you once you are heading in the right direction.*

8

APPROPRIATE GOAL SETTING FOR RECOVERING HIGH-FFs

But have we got the right goals? This remains a core concern for those with a high fear of failure. While keen to avoid near-peg under-achieving, High-FFs have a flawed capacity to differentiate genuine long-term objectives (which we may still be formulating) from inappropriate fear of failure "reach for the stars" long-peg dreams that may be an elaborate form of avoidance. And this can lead to serious errors.

In his book *Destructive Goal Pursuit* (2006), behaviourist D. Christopher Kayes examines inappropriate goal setting by recounting the story of the 1996 Mount Everest expedition that ended with eight people dead and with others requiring amputations. Kayes's claim is that the expedition was flawed from the start due to its goals, which involved expert mountaineers leading a group of mixed-ability adventurers that had paid up to US$65,000 to climb the world's highest mountain. The commercial status of the expedition changed the dynamic of the climb, he states, because many of the climbers believed they were hiring experts that would ensure they achieved their dream of conquering the mountain.

Kayes blamed the disaster on the relentless pursuit of the goal to conquer the summit even after the experienced team leaders could have heeded warning signs that they were running out of time for a safe descent – a phenomenon Kayes called "goalodicy" (i.e. the pursuit of idiotic goals).

Goalodicy has six key characteristics, states Kayes, all of which those with fear of failure will have to navigate:

* A narrowly defined goal (to get to the summit).
* Public expectation (these were ambitious people – including a celebrity writer – concerned about how they were perceived both within and beyond the group).
* Face-saving behaviour (from both the climbers and the leaders who may have ignored danger signals in order to maintain their credibility).
* A dream of an idealized future (of conquering Everest).
* Goal-driven justification (if the goal becomes "everything" it can be used to justify irrational decisions that may be dangerous), and
* A sense of destiny.

"Goalodicy works by allowing teams to put off the reality of the present in the hope that achieving a future goal will eliminate current obstacles," writes Kayes.

Once a team sets a goal, persuading it otherwise can be difficult, states Kayes. And it can be the same for individuals. Goals pull people through and offer a sense of purpose. Yet setting goals that are way too ambitious or ill-considered against what is actually achievable, may inspire more risk taking and make us feel justified in going beyond accepted norms, which can lead to dangerous and even unethical behaviour.

With respect to the Everest climbers, this led to an inability to learn and change as the facts changed around them (their ascent was delayed by bottlenecks and bad weather, which restricted their scope for a safe descent). Their goal was too tight and they were too dependent on one aspect of the pursuit: their leaders, who the followers depended upon as the only people capable of making knowledge-based decisions on whether it was safe to continue.

Setting the wrong goals can be fatal

So what can be learnt from Christopher Kayes's excellent recounting of this fated Everest expedition? A key lesson has to be that the team set the wrong goal, despite the fact the goal appeared obvious. That US$65,000 fee was not for an ascent to the summit of Everest. It was for reaching the summit and making it down again – *alive*! It may have been that crucial narrowing of the goal that led to the disaster because it clouded the judgement of the team leaders, who may have become overly concerned about the implicit promises within the fee. And if this sounds unrealistic – that the revised goal is too wide – compare it to the Apollo moon landings, which had getting the astronauts home as an equal and integral objective (just ask Gene Kranz).

An important point here is that progress for its own sake is not progress, despite the fact it may temporarily energize us. If you are working towards the wrong goal, you are simply setting yourself a trap, which – as in the case of the Everest climbers – can lead to a fatal reckoning. At the very least you are simply wasting your time.

Setting the right goals requires you to return to *Your Constitution*. For instance, my goal of a Norfolk farm and a rare breed of sheep looks pretty hollow without my commitments as a father and husband (or as a farmer, which was absent – suggesting it may not even be *my* goal). If I fail to include my family, a lonely farm in the middle of nowhere is probably the last place I'd like to end up.

You have to make sure that your goals are in balance with the rest of your life. As Julie Starr (2003) states, if you want a job with lots of travel and you have a young family, you need to think through the consequences of achieving that goal. If you are prepared to pay that price, fine. But goal setting based on achievement motivation needs to maintain us through a timeframe that looks well beyond desperate short-term wins that require such an acute level of sacrifice we end up spending the rest of our lives rueing the day we achieved them. That 10-year time horizon is there for a reason.

Money's diminishing returns

Money is a particular problem when trying to set appropriate goals. Wealth is an obvious objective but perspective is required. In *Living the 80/20 Way* (2005) entrepreneur Richard Koch writes that most people over estimate the return they will receive from earning more. Studies show that poverty makes us unhappy, writes Koch, but once we're moderately well off, adding even more money doesn't make us happier and can even add stresses that get in the way of happiness.

Money-based goals also bring other problems – not dissimilar to those faced on Everest. If your goal is to be a millionaire by the time you are 30, what price are you prepared to pay to achieve it? Perhaps you'll sacrifice a social life and put off any relationship or family commitments. You may even be prepared to be a bit of a toady in the office. But are you prepared to shaft the guy in the next cubicle? You are? OK, what about commit fraud? Really – blimey! So where does it end? Robbery, murder, genocide?

Is there no limit to what you'd do to reach that goal? This is the extreme end of High-FF behaviour – the land of the megalomaniac who is so afraid of failure they are willing to go way beyond inappropriate goal setting. Such extremists will find their own *Constitution*, if written honestly, a document dripping with clenched hatred and perceived injustice (Hitler's *Mein Kampf* is a classic example).

Anthony Robbins (1992) warns against abusing ourselves in the pursuit of a single goal – tying our entire level of personal happiness to our ability to achieve goals that may be beyond our control. It is not just achieving the objective that matters but the quality of life we experience along the way, he says, which is why *Our Constitution* needs to be our grounding document and contain our values across the spectrum or our life.

Robbins is convinced that many of us go through life putting off our happiness in order to achieve that next goal. "Someday" seems to be the goal of the permanently unhappy, he says. Yet we should decide to be happy now. Goal setting is not some form of delayed gratification. It is about setting our "compass" – as Covey would say – and being uplifted as we start to walk in the right direction, knowing where we are heading and with the faith to deal with the bends in the road along the way.

"Remember the direction we are heading is more important than the individual results," says Robbins.

Setting goals beyond our goals

Another core component of this is in having goals beyond our goals. One of the key reasons I failed at both investment banking and as a writer is that I had no idea what to do once I'd "made it." I'd not thought about the next stage at all, meaning that I floundered within both roles without any of the focus and drive that won me the opportunities in the first place.

"Never give up setting goals," says Robbins. "Achieving our goals can be a curse unless we have already set higher goals before reaching the first."

The idea of "outrunning" our dreams, as I found out at the bank, can lead to an "is that all" deflation, albeit in a better setting. Lindsey Agness (2008) quotes John Grinder (the co-founder of NLP) stating that the biggest factor stopping goal achievement is often the failure to set goals beyond our initial goal. With no higher level to aim for we can end up sabotaging ourselves the minute the original goal is achieved – exactly what happened to me with both banking and writing.

Hopefully, setting 10-year goals that complement *Your Constitution* – including short-term milestones – should help overcome this problem. *Your Constitution* should create a framework for both your short-term objectives and long-term ambitions. For instance,

Julie Starr's parent wanting energy to play sport with her kids would soon find the badminton sessions losing their appeal unless she could take it to the next stage. Perhaps her real objective was to "stay connected and relevant to my children as they move from childhood to adulthood." As a part of *Her Constitution* it would make the badminton sessions just one part of a programme with a clearly defined, long-term, objective that also contains flexibility and a measurable result.

Importantly, such a statement also avoids being a hostage-to-fortune – such as becoming a millionaire by 30 or summiting Everest at the first attempt. Of those that perished on Everest, surely a better objective would have been "to become an accomplished mountaineer" or even the more constitutional "to maintain my sense of physical adventure throughout my life."

If we could have our goals now – would we?

Another way of checking whether we are heading in the right direction is to adopt another one of Julie Starr's methodologies from *The Coaching Manual*. If you could have your goal now, she asks, would you take it? If there are any caveats to prevent you immediately and whole-heartedly shouting "*YES,*" you may need to examine why this is the case.

If, for instance, you visualized yourself running a company of 100 people and – offered the opportunity to do so – hesitate or even panic at the thought, it may be that such a goal is no more than a fantasy (perhaps given to you by someone else or by conditioning). Maybe a goal more tailored to your well-being would be running a smaller team of, say, five, but in a collegiate studio setting, maybe in a town with a more human scale.

Of course, the 100 person company may well be appropriate as a 10-year goal after a good baptism of fire involving a company with fewer employees. Having said this, your terror at the thought of running such a company now should also have an impact on your 10, five or two-year goals, and even on *Your Constitution*.

We need to concentrate on being who *we* are. Most of the Everest climbers were not professional mountaineers – many were disastrously ill-prepared for climbing a mountain that was climbed for the first time *ever* only in 1953 (at least officially).

"If you have a lemon, make lemonade," wrote Dale Carnegie (1948), meaning we should look at what we have and what we can do with it.

This is not advocating that changes in direction are ill-advised. It is simply stating that aiming to become a mathematics professor when it is obvious we are more of the creative-writer type will massively increase our chances of failure and further disappointment. And that will reinforce rather than counter our negative self-beliefs.

Recognize the milestones

A final element that can scupper the progress we make from goal setting is in becoming so caught up in the process of goal achievement that we fail to observe how far we have come. Progress can creep up on us to the point where we ignore it, which means we maintain the negative feelings we had before we started and fail to look at past achievements as building blocks for the future. This is a crucial failing of the High-FF and can result in our progress towards our goals having no impact on our general well-being. In some respects this is inevitable – we are who we are. Those neural hijackings are not going to disappear.

However, just as we can learn to refute the hijackings more and more quickly, so we can learn – over time – that the feelings we have are false and that those tiny steps of progress towards our goals should start to build our confidence and reduce our fears. Keeping a diary helps – not least because it means we have to rewrite our 10-year objectives annually, allowing us to monitor progress and record the achieved milestones (perhaps with a big tick). And the annually renewed 10-year horizon means we never "outrun" our goals.

Importantly, a diary also allows you to annually renew *Your Constitution*. This is not a contradiction in terms. *Your Constitution* is far from carved in stone. Like the *U.S. Constitution* (which has 26 amendments) *Your Constitution* is a working document that, to remain relevant, has to reflect your current values and absorb new realities (getting married, changed mine for instance). Of course, the hurdles for change should be high or you may have no intention of living by the values you state. Yet that transfer moment to a new diary allows you some room for thought and some gentle recrafting, although wholesale rewritings are unadvisable (simply because new values may quickly fade).

Case Study 8 – Looking beyond the immediate

Since sending me an email after reading *What's Stopping You?* I've been in regular correspondence with a young American actress called Libby. From her *YouTube* clippings I could see she was talented. But she suffered from a terrible fear of failure, she said, although told me such an affliction was rife within the acting community.

"We're all inwardly convinced we're terrible," she wrote. "We all think the other actors are better than we are. And that they are just humouring us, although probably being critical behind our backs."

Her personal pain was particularly deep, however, as she suffered from bouts of depression, or what she called that "bluesy feeling" – the latest being due to a rejection from an agent who'd taken on a friend.

"Talk about a victory for the monkey!" she exclaimed.

We got into discussions about long-term goals and she was soon attempting the 10-year visualization exercise.

The results surprised her.

"The timeline is so interesting because I looked through all the actressy stuff and beyond it – and I realized it wasn't being an actress that inspired me, it was being in film. It was the movie business I loved, not acting."

Over the next few days Libby kept returning to her visualization – adding details to her originally sketchy thoughts of being a film director, as well as thinking about the milestones.

"I'm now convinced I have the answer," she wrote to me later and – within a month – she wrote again, excitedly relating that she'd written a short film, found an assistant director, a producer and had a readthrough of her first short movie.

Of course, I warned her there would be setbacks – not least rejections – ahead. Yet, with her energies pointed towards what she thought a more productive pursuit – and one that married well with her long-term objectives – she felt more than capable of coping with the difficulties she knew lay ahead.

What's Stopping You? *You need to ensure that your goals complement who you are. You also need goals beyond your initial goals. And you need to recognize the progress you make along the way.*

PART THREE
Execution

9

STRATEGY AND TACTICS

Objectives, strategy, tactics. That's our order at *Moorgate* when planning a PR campaign. And it seems perfectly applicable as a route for execution when developing achievement motivation in individuals with a high fear of failure. So with the objectives written, we need to move to the next stage: establishing our "strategy," although this immediately presents us with a problem. What – exactly – is a strategy?

The dictionary definition states it is the "art or science of the planning and conduct of a war," which is helpful but too broad for me and, I suspect, many recovering High-FFs. We can be easily put off by ambiguities, with even the meaning of a word sometimes enough to halt our progress. And while many books have been written with the word strategy in the title, nearly all assume an understanding of the word and then promptly mix strategy and tactics without any recognition of their different roles in the pursuit of our goals.

"In order for a goal to be attainable, it must be *operationally defined*," says Phillip C. McGraw, the author of *Life Strategies* (1999), which seemed the most obvious self-help book to consult because it was aimed at individuals rather than businesses.

The italics on "operationally defined" are mine because it jumped out at me as a possible definition of strategy, although – again – an operational definition could become confused with the practical day-to-day tactics and action points we employ.

The strategic bridge

After toying with this conundrum for a while I realized that, even in our PR campaigns, we tend to use the "strategy" section of our *Campaign Plan* – our key execution document that gives the client confidence regarding our aims for the campaign and the steps we are taking to achieve them – as a chance to summarize the objectives before translating them into relevant tactics and action points. In other words the strategy bridges the client's goals and our actual actions – ensuring that our tactics (i.e. the executable action points) are focused on meeting the objectives. And this, to me, is the perfect definition of a strategy.

As a bridge between the objectives and the executable tactics, the strategy is therefore vital. For military planners trying to achieve their objective (victory) one strategy could be to execute "total war" – attacking by land, sea and air. This may seem like an obvious strategy in war, but it isn't. Alternative strategies could be to wait for an opponent's onslaught or operate a guerrilla campaign in enemy territory (yet even here we can quickly see tactical language slipping in). So a strategy of "total war" may lead, tactically, to the employment of company A – backed up by warship B and air squadron C – to storm beach X in month Y.

At *Moorgate* we have found that settling on a strategy for the client can be the most difficult part of a campaign – not least because it can seem so obvious at the start. Obvious strategies – like winning a war using the army, navy and air force – can result in objectives melding into tactics too readily, with potentially disastrous results.

For instance, a common objective in public relations is to generate warm sales leads for our clients. Most clients assume that such an objective translates into a strategy of generating news coverage via tactics such as writing and distributing news releases before lobbying for coverage in the press. But is such a strategy correct? Well that depends on the client. If our client is a challenger in the sector, perhaps just launching its offering, then a strategy of building public profile by generating news articles over a period of months will surely work best.

But what if the client is the entrenched market leader and is fending off the challengers? Perhaps the strategy here should be to profile their track-record, which would encourage tactics such as writing opinion-pieces or profile articles, or maybe case studies of happy customers. In both scenarios the tactics employed are very much a product of a strategy developed to suit the client's strengths (and weaknesses), which differ greatly despite the identical objective.

This is important because, as Steven Silbiger says in *The 10 Day MBA* (1993), "strategic plans cannot be formed in a vacuum. They must fit organizations just as marketing plans must be suited to products," which is in line with our need as individuals to undertake a campaign for progress that takes account of our strengths and weaknesses.

Advantages of a strategy

And there are other benefits to having a strategy, as outlined by Robert S. Kaplan in *The Execution Premium* (2008):

"Strategic initiatives represent the force that accelerates an organizational mass [or individual] into action, overcoming inertia and resistance to change," making the strategy the key element for injecting momentum into our pursuits.

Indeed, in *Life Strategies* McGraw points out that having a strategy frees us from a "pointless and misguided reliance on willpower," which he considers a myth – "an unreliable emotional fuel, experienced at fever pitch."

Willpower will temporarily energize our efforts, he says – helping us to make the leap – but it will also bring us to a halt once the emotional responses to our early progress are spent. This makes willpower a dangerous energizer for High-FFs too used to being driven by their emotions and insecurities. Far better, says McGraw, to develop and execute a well-defined strategy – especially one that manages to remove our emotions as key drivers.

And Kaplan and Silbiger's references to organizations point to another strength of having a strategy – our chance to depersonalize our goal-seeking endeavours. As stated in Part One, this is not about us as people. It is about us achieving our goals, which stand outside of any judgement about who we are. Depersonalization allows us to think of ourselves as companies – as *Me Inc.* – which means we are focused on achieving our objectives by developing a strategy and employing suitable tactics rather than focused on our concerns regarding how our actions look to outsiders. Such a focus clearly aids our judgement because we are no longer interpreting every bump in the road as a personal and final verdict, which also prevents setbacks from sabotaging our decision-making.

The strength of adopting "objectives, strategy, tactics"

Sorry to labour the point, but outlining a strategy offers one final strength. As stated, at *Moorgate* we execute PR campaigns after first recording the strategy on a *Campaign Plan* that also contains the objectives, tactics and – as we are a PR company – the audiences and messages. The client then agrees all this and we execute. Yet if our tactics do not produce the desired results we can work our way back up the document, first questioning and replacing the tactics while assuming the strategy fine. Then, if this fails, we can reassess whether we have the right strategy, and finally we can re-evaluate the objectives.

We therefore have a structural confidence that allows us to execute without any nagging doubts regarding the achievability of the objective, which is put in its place at the very top of our *Campaign Plan*. Only after repeated tactical failures do we look at the strategy. And only after repeated strategic failures would we begin to question the achievability of the objectives.

There is a tremendous strength in recovering High-FFs adopting such an approach in my opinion. Tactical failures are simply action points that failed to produce the desired result. Yet those with fear of failure interpret even minor setbacks as affirmation of their inner and irretrievable awfulness. Not only is this patently untrue – a conclusion based purely on perception (although a potentially self-fulfilling one) – such a conclusion is impossible if we have, first, depersonalized our goals as part of a *Me Inc.* project and, second, divorced our strategy and tactics from our objectives so that setbacks in execution do not derail our progress towards our goals.

The war *will* be won. It is just a question of how.

The SWOT

So how do we determine the right strategy? As stated, we must tailor our strategy to our strengths and weaknesses, so these need to be assessed. One method we use for our clients is to first undertake a SWOT (strengths, weaknesses, opportunities, threats) analysis, which we add to the *Campaign Plan*. SWOTs are also advocated by *Harvard Business School*, no less, in its book *Strategy* (2005), which again invokes the war analogy – stating that even the best battle plan is useless unless commanders understand whether their soldiers can carry it out. And this needs to take strengths and limitations into account.

From the SWOT we usually find that the strategy becomes clear, as it will tell us about our readiness for execution, our knowledge regarding the resources required and whether we have those resources to hand. It will also alert us to issues that may arise to destabilize us, as well as alternative tactics we can employ or consider employing – perhaps being opportunistic (previously the realm of those with high achievement motivation).

Again, this can work for individuals as well as companies. Certainly it worked for me when I set up *Moorgate*. My strategy needed to take account of the fact I had not one jot of PR experience and knew no one in the PR industry, but that I had strong journalistic skills and "good" experience in banking.

The objective was obvious – to create a successful financial PR agency starting with the major banks (the entities I best understood) as clients. But what then? I did a SWOT analysis and it was from this that the obvious strategy emerged, although one that would have remained hidden without such an exercise.

It went something like this:

Strengths
- A strong background in financial journalism and magazine editing.
- "Good" experience in banking – especially corporate and investment banking (UK/US).
- Lots of contacts in banking and financial journalism.
- Some experience in entrepreneurialism.
- A strong desire to stop failing at things.

Weaknesses
- No actual PR experience, or track-record.
- US-experience meant my London contact-base was old.
- Lack of self-belief has been my historical undoing.
- Other multiple debilitating insecurities caused by a negative and persistent monkey residing on my back.

Opportunities
- As an editor I remember being irritated by ill-informed PRs – surely a well-informed PR would get a better response?
- Many big PR agencies court the banks but neglect corporate banking, despite the size of that market. This is partly because of its complexity – it is aimed at highly sophisticated financial directors.
- This neglect has left many corporate bankers doing their own PR – including me when I was a banker (so, in fact, I do have some PR experience – I'd just discounted it). But they need help.

- I am in a strong position to start an agency because I ran an incubator for start-ups, which is being sold.

Threats
- The incubator may close before I have time to establish *Moorgate*.
- Rivals may catch on and do it themselves – especially given that our target clients will all have currently contracted PR agencies.
- I may hate it.

A strategy based on strengths and opportunities

So the obvious strategy emerged – focus on my former area of corporate banking using my strong journalistic skills as bait for those now struggling to execute their own PR. And the fact I had no track record in PR was irrelevant given my other experiences – in fact, given how poorly the existing PR agencies had performed in this area, it was an advantage.

A clear weakness, however, was my eroded contact base – a major failing for a PR. Yet having identified this as a weakness, I was able to direct my medium-term tactics (see below) in that direction. I contacted the few people I still knew in London and wangled meetings just to discuss the PR idea. I also accepted any offer to attend conferences or drinks parties and, importantly, kept networking after half the people I spoke to raised an eyebrow regarding my plans and excused themselves. Half the room didn't, so I focused on them, especially the banker who started complaining about having to do his own marketing – including writing articles for English language magazines despite being Dutch.

In fact the SWOT led to one tactical mistake – which it could have also prevented had I paid it proper attention. The lack of contacts, and my specialist knowledge, fooled me into thinking I could approach other PR agencies and suggest a "white label" service for them to offer their existing clients. So focused was I on blind activity that I emailed a dozen or so agencies asking for a meeting and, of course, those that were to become my closest rivals were more than happy for me to reveal my plan for wrestling business away from them.

Had I known more about the PR industry I would have known that – like male Siamese Fighting Fish – no two agencies can ever be in the same room without trying to kill each other, which means handing over intellectual property to the competition is potentially suicidal. Yet my closest rivals failed to see how they were under-serving the sector so didn't change their behaviour – meaning they didn't catch-on to the potential of our methodology until *Moorgate* was well-established.

Be different

And, of course, without realizing it I'd hit upon a key strategic concept when starting a business: differentiation – a concept that works just as well for individuals.

"Specialization lines up where the world is going," says renowned corporate strategist Jack Trout in his book *Trout on Strategy* (2004) stating that we should offer a key "point of differentiation" from others (including our peers) to establish our brand in the customer's (or our boss's) mind.

What are the trends in our area or targeted area, including our career or company? Where is that world heading? What is done badly? Why? How can it be improved? What are the barriers to this improvement? What role can *we* play? Do we want that role? If yes, what's our strategy for achieving this?

But differentiation requires self-belief, especially when – as in my case – half the people we approach think we are crazy (often those with the most experience in a particular area). Yet experience executing PR as a banker – as well as my misguided meetings with other agencies – gave me the self-belief to realize my detractors didn't matter. In fact they were the ones that persuaded me of the gap in the market for financial PR that didn't involve blond bobs, dazzle-white teeth and flirty smiles (none of which I possessed).

Actually, I was grateful for their presence as they provided a strong benchmark for my differentiation. I could turn what I was not into a positive. Indeed, Steve Chandler (2001) encourages us to "exploit our weaknesses."

We should turn the traits, tendencies and characteristics we most dislike about ourselves into signature assets, he says, citing Arnold Schwarzenegger who used his Austrian accent as a selling point for the movies and being a political outsider as a vote winner for politics.

The "jumping out of the aeroplane" moment

And with the strategy decided we can move towards tactical execution – actually storming beach X in month Y. Researching the market for the right organization to work for is a tactic. A job application is a tactic. Developing a contact base in a particular industry is a tactic. Tactics are our immediate action points towards meeting our goals – often clustered under various headings such as relationship building, skill acquisition or research. They represent a big moment. This is the recovering High-FF's equivalent of jumping out of the aeroplane and no amount of instruction, training and parachute-checking is going to take away the terror of that moment.

In fact, the preparation *is* our parachute. It will allow us to act – not least because in developing our strategy the next steps should appear logical if not obvious. An important point of principle here is that we must do what feels like the most logical next step. Have faith that the seemingly obvious thing to do is almost certainly the right next move – not least because it will be the product of all that planning. This is the moment we pull the lever on our machine, so the widget that comes out the bottom should, of course, look familiar.

"Simplicity is the first principle."

At least that's the advice of Sun Tze's *Art of War*, as applied to business in *Sun Tzu for Execution* by US entrepreneur and Sun Tze enthusiast Steven W. Michaelson (2006). "If execution is more complicated than it needs to be it won't be as successful," he writes, while ". . . simple ideas, executed with gusto, have a tendency to work. And they work despite their shortcomings."

It doesn't take long for most business books discussing tactics to start quoting this famous Chinese war-focused philosopher. Yet Michaelson's is an excellent application of Sun Tze's philosophy because it focuses on execution. For instance he states that size is unimportant – "the battle doesn't always go to the side with the biggest army" – while preparation is key, as is seizing a favourable position beforehand – "for Sun Tze a favourable position gave control over the battlefield." Attitude is also important – "a positive attitude wins over a negative one" – as is speed – "speed is the essence of war" and opportunism – "if the enemy leaves a door open, you must rush in."

The required fight

Sun Tze – especially as translated by Michaelson – can put fire in our bellies for the battles ahead. But it may not work for everyone, especially as many High-FFs have poor experience of battles. Those with a high fear of failure often "retire hurt" from such fights feeling as if they have been tactically outmanoeuvred and physically outgunned, probably by someone who spends their evenings reading Sun Tze. Indeed, going back to those Atkinson-style experiments, battles are the very thing High-FFs hate most, making battle analogies off-putting when it comes to motivation.

Yet we are our own worst enemy in this respect. We are trying to beat our inner demons to make progress in our lives. And this requires fight. We cannot be pacifists in this endeavour. We *will* face external competition, whatever our goals. There are many applicants for every promotion or job, many companies vying for the business of our potential clients, many rivals for the attentions of our intended personal conquests. And we have rolled over too many times already in our lives.

Giving way to those High-AMs because, what the hell, they were bound to win in the end, is no longer a viable option. It is self-fulfilling defeatism that has no place in the thinking of a recovering High-FF. This is the point where we make our stand. So there is no escaping the fact we have a battle on our hands (although as we shall see, not all battles involve a win–lose outcome). And, in this respect, Sun Tze seems pretty apt in helping us mentally prepare.

Rules for tactical execution

If we are therefore reconciled to battle, how do we align our forces and move onwards to victory? What rules can we set for our tactics at this point to ensure they support our strategy? Indeed, what can all the testosterone-fuelled philosophies of Sun Tze offer us in today's environment, where charging around an office dressed as a sword-wielding Chinese warrior is unlikely to be seen as appropriate behaviour?

As ever, I searched the business and personal texts for the definitive answers. But then I jotted down my own and thought these as strong as anything I could find from reading all those books:

- Tactics are nothing more than a series of moves aimed at meeting our objectives. Most often they are moves arranged in a linear form (i.e. one after the other).
- Tactics are mostly action points – contact this person, write this letter, make that phone call, get that meeting. But they can also be developmental – find out about that course, develop this skill.

- In fact you should organize your tactics under a series of headings, such as: research, skill acquisition, relationship building – or something more immediate such as applications, contacts, books to read, etc.
- Tactics can be tiny steps or giant leaps. Giant leaps are rare, however, and can often move you to the wrong place. In fact, where possible, giant leaps should be converted into a series of tiny steps that produce a series of small victories.
- Planned action points need to involve both the next steps and the second series of steps after the first milestones have been reached.
- Immediate tactics should focus on your strengths while medium-term tactics can look towards overcoming your weaknesses.
- Those looking at over-coming weaknesses should focus on gathering information or on acquiring skills for medium-term milestones.
- Execution tactics are only for where we have the strength to act. Bold leaps based purely on bravado are pointless, potentially wasteful and should be avoided.
- Don't execute tactics on too many fronts. Concentrate energies in one place in order to gain small victories. And then move on.
- Use your diary to determine deadlines, calculate priorities, assess your outcomes and record your (small) victories (and setbacks).
- Deadlines should be the key determinant of the order in which you tackle the action points, although make sure each action moves you towards your goal and that key deadlines are not being missed elsewhere that may be more important for your objectives.
- Work out the cost (in every respect – mental, financial, social, physical) of each tactic beforehand and be prepared to pay it. Baulking at the cost halfway through is the quickest way to derail an entire campaign.
- In fact, factor in some overspend – it is bound to happen.

- Don't start a tactic without a clear idea of its outcome, and focus purely on that outcome – most alternative outcomes will, in reality, be setbacks.
- But be flexible. As the Prussian field marshal Helmuth von Moltke said: "No plan survives contact with the enemy" – meaning that, while our desired outcome should not be compromised, our route to achieving it may require rapid revision as we execute.

Case Study 9 – A "degree in self-sabotage"

David approached me seeking career guidance after claiming he has a "degree in self-sabotage."

"I literally have a person inside me working against my own success," he wrote.

He was outwardly successful, with a PhD in computer science and a 20-year career in IT. Yet he dismissed these achievements in favour of a negative internal assessment in which the professors took pity on him or that, out of fear, he was the only person willing to do the job.

He claimed to be well organized and not lacking in direction. But he was incapable of making positive leaps.

"The most self-sabotaging trait I possess is procrastination," he stated. "I take zero financial risks and I avoid publicizing my academic work because of the fear of criticism. Even my successes are tempered by the feeling that I have failed to take advantage of the situation."

I could offer no easy way out for David. There is no button to press that will remove poor self-beliefs, although I was keen to explore further his self-sabotaging. He claimed that he would literally "telescope" his perceived weaknesses in interviews.

"I noticed that I was advertising my weaknesses by starting statements like 'one thing you should know is that I'm not particularly good at . . . ,'" he said. "Although it seems bizarre in hindsight, I was unaware I was doing this at first. On reflection I realized it was my fear of potentially being humiliated that led me to literally hand the interviewers a guide to my perceived shortcomings."

Yet his awareness of this was a major step forward. Soon he was emailing me saying he had completed the five-, two- and one-year milestones of his visualized future, and that this had already made a difference in interviews because his applications felt more like the obvious next step. They no longer felt like a leap into the unknown, in which the interviewer held all the cards and his only hope was a "take pity on me" confession.

And he'd developed one very effective tactic for overcoming his biggest weakness.

"I've decided to proactively do things that have a large chance of failure," he wrote. "For instance, I recently undertook a gruelling technical test for a potential post. I would have previously run a mile, but I decided it would be good practice – helping me get over my fear of such assessments. In fact I aced it, making me realize that my fear of failure had caused me to exaggerate the possibility of failure."

What's Stopping You? *After goal-setting you need to develop a strategy – the bridge that ensures your tactical action points are focused on your objectives. Your strategy needs to take account of your strengths and weaknesses. Tactics, meanwhile, are the tiny steps you take daily – allowing small victories to build into significant progress.*

10

JUDGEMENT AND IDEAS

Good judgement is the key to executing any plan. We need the ability to make the right decisions at the right moments. Yet those with a high fear of failure struggle with respect to judgement. For instance, how many times are we told to make decisions relying on our gut instinct when, as High-FFs, our gut instinct may be derived from fear, insecurities and perceived slights and prejudices against us? For the recovering High-FF, gut instinct is something we may have to ignore or overcome in order to make strong decisions.

In *Judgement* (2007) leadership academics Noel M. Tichy and Warren G. Bennis state that solid judgement requires a good character and a strong internal "moral compass," both of which – as High-FFs – we may feel we lack. Yet strong long-term goals and a thought-through strategy offer us the most powerful possible benchmarks for our decisions – making any judgements not about us but about the pursuit of our goals. And if we divide our activities into objectives, strategies and tactics, we are capable of making decisions at a lower level that – no matter what the outcome – should have no immediate bearing at the higher level.

Judgement calls in three stages

According to Tichy and Bennis, judgement calls are made in three stages. There is the "pre" stage, which is in discerning the actual judgement required – "framing and naming" the judgement needed. This is followed by the "call" in which the decision is made, although we first gather as much information as we need, which may lead to the realization that we do not have enough information or need to enlist different people. And finally there is the "execution," which is making our decision happen. This requires commitment.

And if this sounds like a recipe for protracted decision making: so be it. Strong decisions take time to get right, especially for the recovering High-FF with a past wrecked by poor decision-making.

"Good judgement is not one terrific *aha* moment after another," write Tichy and Bennis. "In the real world, good judgement, at least on the big issues that make a difference, is usually an incremental process."

This chimes well with Stephen Covey (1989) who states that the best way to improve our responses is to focus on the distance "between stimulus and response." If we can lengthen this distance our decisions will be less focused on our emotions (a common High-FF trait) and more focused on achieving our goals, which should produce better results.

The joy of crises

Tichy and Bennis also state that decision-making is in three domains: judgements about people, judgements about strategy, and judgements in times of crisis. We will deal with people later and have already dealt with strategy in the previous chapter – so what about judgements in a crisis?

Crises are the moments for the recovering High-FF to step out of the shadows and step up to the plate – not least because the potential for humiliation has been removed. Failed is the current state – our worst-case scenario has arrived – allowing the High-FF to take humiliation-free risks, which takes us back to Gene Kranz and his "failure is not an option" moment.

Certainly, we must take responsibility for dealing with a crisis when it comes. Blame can wait for calmer moments, although we should thank those responsible for giving us the opportunity to make strong decisions from (usually) a depersonalized perspective.

According to Steve Chandler (2001) we should look for the gift within every problem. For instance, in public relations the most regular crisis we face is an unhappy client. If the cause is external – some poor publicity perhaps – then the crisis will strengthen their dependence on us. We are the fire brigade arriving just in time to put out the flames and direct the clean up (usually involving a nice lunch with the offending journalist in order to "re-educate" them). If the crisis is internal – they are unhappy with us – then this is usually a good opportunity to go back to the *Campaign Plan*, reassess the tactics and (after repeated tactical failures) ensure we have the right strategy.

If the problem really is with *us* then it is often a chance for me to step in and show my team what I can do to soothe a client's anger. I can take charge of a project or return to the fore with respect to running the account, which will do my stock little harm with both my employees and the client. If even that fails and we lose the account – which is rare given the structural strength of our *Campaign Plans* – we then have a major opportunity to learn from our mistakes and perhaps reshuffle the team.

50:50s

A final point on judgement deals with those 50:50 choices – especially when it isn't always apparent which route best supports our long-term objectives. Deciding between closely aligned university places, career paths, job-offers, promotions or even potential employees are key moments in our life and they can, for the High-FF, trigger fear-based insecurities that lead to false evaluations and major mistakes, or indecision at best. If life comes down to a handful of decisions, these are them – and they are usually the moments, above all else, that provide the monkey with all the evidence he needs regarding our innate awfulness.

There is no easy way of dealing with such decisions, and no way of completely removing the fear. My own method has been to draw two columns headed by our choices – say UEA or UCL – with the rows the factors that will influence my decision, which for universities would include such things as: structure of course, course reputation, college reputation, city, distance from home, other friends attending, nightlife and accommodation. We then need to score each and, importantly, weight each (perhaps banding a few of the peripherals – such as city and nightlife – together). And if it gives us the result we didn't want, then the exercise at least helps confirm the choice we favour.

And importantly we should not regret the decision. Regret is a major trait of the High-FF, with us spending much of our lives pondering parallel universes, "if only" we'd made this or that choice. Of course, the rival world is always the one in which we have achieved our goals and lost our fears, leaving us cursing our poor decision-making or hesitancy regarding opportunities. Meanwhile, our purgatory continues in the real world – with those regrets piling up just beyond every decision-requiring crossroads.

Yet regretting the unknown is madness. It is self-inflicted torture and a cheap victory for the monkey. And it is easily refuted, simply because we are – indeed – High-FFs. As stated, the insecurities that dog High-FFs are innate. There is no decision or outcome that will remove our fears, so the feelings we have now we'd still have – even if we'd made all the right decisions and achieved all our wildest dreams (as stated, an insight into celebrity behaviour is all the evidence required to prove this point).

And we must remember that each lifespan involves multiple 50:50 moments. Sheer probability tells us that we'll get some right and some wrong, so it is self-defeating to simply focus on those we potentially (but not certainly) got wrong.

Of course, as High-FFs such balanced thinking is a stretch, so we could always focus on the fact that, "knowing our luck," we'd have probably been run over by a bus on the first day along the alternative road.

The false hope of ideas

Like judgements, ideas are key execution tool. And, again, they are a problematic area for those handicapped with a high fear of failure. Many High-FFs are very good at generating ideas, although most High-FFs fall at the first hurdle when it comes to implementation. Over time, this renders us incapable of differentiating between good and bad ideas, which – sadly – leaves us haunted by our creativity (especially when we see our ideas being implemented by others). For those with a high fear of failure ideas can seem like pipe-dreams, often giving us nothing more than false hope and an additional layer of frustration.

Other High-FFs, however, can struggle to think imaginatively – perhaps because, so trapped are they in their current status, they have switched off their creative brain. So while the sensitivity of the High-FF lends itself to creativity, poor experiences may mean we have extinguished the flame or – potentially worse – become tormented by our own ideas.

And this is bad news when trying to implement a strategy for meeting our objectives because navigating the inevitable "rocks in the river" (to quote Robbins) requires strong imagination as well as strong judgement.

According to advertising executive Jack Foster in *How to Get Ideas* (1996) people who come up with good ideas know they exist and know they will find them, which can, initially, seem unhelpful. What if we are not confident good ideas exist? If Foster states that the most important factor needed for successful idea generation is self-belief, then those without it are surely doomed, at least in terms of idea generation.

But there is hope. For Foster the key problem is being a grown up. Adults think too much. They are hampered by experience, which – for those with a high fear of failure – is usually negative experience. Boundaries, rules, fears: all crowd in on the adult trying to generate ideas.

So the answer is to be more like children. As children we all indulged in imaginative play without rules or boundaries, so we need – once again – to tap into that childlike freedom of illogical and silly creativity.

"Kids are natural born scientists," says Foster, quoting astronomer Carl Sagan. "First of all they ask the deep scientific questions. Why is the moon round? . . . By the time they get into High School they hardly ever ask questions like that."

For the High-FF, this is because the fear of failure has kicked in – with all the attendant concerns regarding public humiliation.

Yet nearly all children go through the "why" stage, and we should do our best to return to that wonderfully creative period when young eyes are looking and articulating thoughts and ideas for the first time.

In fact this is highly possible for the High-FF. As stated, High-FFs are often sensitive types that have ideas but then fear the criticism airing such ideas may bring. Yet this is no different to any creative: designers, writers, artists are all overly sensitive to criticism. The difference between them and us (as High-FFs) is that they manage to overcome their fears. How? By pursuing strong objectives via well-thought through strategies and well-executed tactics. This has meant that their RAS is tuned to their creativity, not their sensitivity.

High-FFs, meanwhile, are tuned incorrectly, which either blocks creativity totally or paralyzes any potential our creativity generates. With our RAS set to goal-achievement, however, our ideas are likely to be more useful to our positive pursuits, rather than our darkest contemplations.

A technique for producing ideas

James Webb Young is the Sun Tze of ideas. And in his 1960s book *A Technique for Producing Ideas* he set out what he saw as a strong process for advertising creatives to follow when trying to think up campaigns in that burgeoning industry.

"The production of ideas is just as definite a process as the production of Fords," was Webb Young's view.

He stated that there were general principles that underpinned the production of ideas, and that these included the notion that ideas are, more or less, "a new combination of old elements." This is not dissimilar to a comedian's thought process (Foster suggests we study comedians if we are struggling to think like children) and, like the comic, the key need is the ability to see relationships between different elements in order to create a new (perhaps funny) version of reality.

Webb Young followed this up with a simple and intuitive step-by-step methodology:

- Gather *all* the "raw materials" relating to your immediate problem – both general and specific.
- Store them in a way that allows for easy and quick reference (this means visually rather than electronically). He suggests writing notes on those classic 6×4 inch indexing cards or in a scrap book.
- Mull over the information – play with it, read it again and again. Notice different – not necessarily relevant – aspects of the information.
- Incubate this information. Go and do something else (Webb Young cites Sherlock Holmes always taking the rational and irritated Watson to a concert halfway through a case).
- Come back to the information afresh and look for the "eureka" moment.
- Develop the idea into its final shape – perhaps asking others to evaluate it.

But what if this only throws up rotten ideas? According to Foster there is no such thing as a bad idea. As with Thomas Edison and his experiments with light-bulbs/rubber, bad ideas are no more than part of the elimination process for the creation of good ideas. And some bad ideas are not bad ideas at all – they just haven't been judged correctly. For instance, Richard Drew – the inventor of Scotch tape (as *Sellotape* is known in the US) – was told to "take this tape . . . and shove it" by the person first trialling it.

Yet we need to be aware that no ideas are final. For every good idea we have there is, according to Foster, an even better one out there. This should motivate us to supplement our ideas with refinements and additions but also to quickly replace our weaker ideas with new and stronger ones. In fact, as long as we are thinking of ideas, we are in the correct frame of mind for thinking up the right idea.

Case Study 10 – Clearing the emotional fog

Soon after *What's Stopping You?* was published I became involved in an intense email exchange with an American woman, Bethany, who'd read my first book. She was enquiring about British male behaviour – particularly with respect to our attitude towards American women. She'd become entangled with a British man while he was living in the States, and remained attached to him even though he'd moved back to London.

On his most recent visit, however, he'd confessed he was now married, although wanted the relationship to continue as he was regularly in the US on business. She was confused by this and, trying to work through her emotions, decided to ask someone who'd previously written about British men "behaving badly" in the US, although was now – I hasten to add – a reformed character (and aware of the insecurities that drove such behaviour).

I was tempted to write back insisting she immediately dump him. But it was obvious she loved him and that she needed to find a way of making that decision herself. And I was also totally ignorant of *his* circumstances – so care was needed.

I asked her to write *Her Constitution*, which she did – including words such as integrity, values, fairness and judgement. I then asked her to visualize herself in 10 years. This soon came back – involving a large family, a shaggy dog, a detached home in the suburbs and a senior position at her international marketing agency. Crucially it did not involve him.

"I stopped replying to his emails," she declared a month or so later. "It wasn't that I was mad at him. Indeed it was painful letting him go. But I knew what I had to do. He was not on my path and that was all that mattered."

What's Stopping You? *Strong goal-setting and a thought-through strategy help you make better judgements that are free of typical High-FF insecurities. They also free your creativity, helping you produce strong ideas that can help your tactical progress.*

11

MANAGING THE PROCESS

"Manage the process" was a line delivered to me by my then future, now former, boss. While a financial journalist, he invited me to give a speech on the competitive landscape of corporate banking at his bank's annual offsite.

Motivated to deliver my first-ever speech involving my specialist knowledge to a group of actual practitioners I worked long and hard to get the presentation right and to deliver it perfectly. There was also the sniff of a job in the air.

On the day, I spent all morning in my hotel room practising in front of the mirror and then did everything I could to mentally prepare myself, including going for a swim just prior to the speech to help me appear relaxed and authoritative. Boy was I prepared, although not for the midday lockout from my room with my notes either inside or in the cleaner's trash – all because I'd forgotten to request an extended check out.

In fact I'd ignored the warning from the organizers that this would happen – being too focused on the speech to take any notice of practical or pressing considerations.

"Manage the process, *laddie*," my future boss said as I tripped in to the lecture hall late and flustered from my desperate and overly emotional exchanges with the cleaning supervisor. The notes had not been trashed, but had been "tidied," so I was terrified throughout that I'd be flummoxed by each new slide, meaning my delivery was nervous and poor.

My great speech had been ruined, not least by my future boss's patronizing comment. In fact I quietly resented it. As comments go it was hardly aimed at easing my nerves. Yet this didn't stop me adopting the motto for my own team in future years. While its wisdom was obvious, it had that all-important edge of superiority about it that I enjoyed. It sounded like something a boss should say to a flustered subordinate – one over-burdened with the expectations of his or her superiors without any of their advantages (PAs, support systems, first-class tickets – years of experience).

But whatever its inadequacy as an encouragement to a team member, it's a useful mantra for us when trying to organize our lives for achievement motivation. This is about getting the small stuff right. About organizing ourselves in such a way that allows time and space for the execution of our strategy and tactics. This is the bit where we overcome mental hurdles such as "I just haven't the time" or "I'm too busy" or "I'm just too disorganized."

Anyone can adopt efficient practices

So what's meant by "managing the process?" To my future/former boss it meant no more than "work out what has to be done, when, and do it." And there may be little need to add more to the definition, except to offer the view that time-and-task management is not a skill, or a talent, or even a craft. It is, indeed, a process. There is nothing innate about efficiency. Anyone can adopt efficient practices – we just have to set ourselves up to be efficient, follow that through, and then turn that process into a habit.

"Getting control of your time means facing up to the fact that you are usually the problem, not someone else," says time-management guru Alec MacKenzie in *The Time Trap* (1972), the mother of all time-management books. "It means doing the hard work of changing well-established habits. It means holding your ground against the negative tugs of human nature."

MacKenzie talks of human characteristics that contradict the laws of time management – such as ego, the desire to please, the fear of offending and the fear of new challenges – all of which are well known to those with a high fear of failure. We may think controlling our work environment is beyond us. Yet giving in to outside pressures is something that resides within *us*, says MacKenzie – using the example of answering the phone when we are busy and then blaming the caller for the interruption.

Covey's four activity boxes

So how can we clear the clutter from our path towards progress? By first clearing the clutter from our thinking.

According to Stephen Covey (1989) every activity in our waking hours belongs in one of four boxes (or "quadrants") in what he calls the "time management matrix." This important-sounding concept simply suggests that all activities are either "urgent" or "not urgent" and – additionally – that all activities are either "important" or "not important."

In my (slightly altered) version the boxes are labelled:

- *Box 1* – urgent and important,
- *Box 2* – urgent and not important,
- *Box 3* – not urgent and important,
- *Box 4* – not urgent and not important.

Covey contends that we spend most of our time on activities in one of the two "urgent" boxes – marked either "important" or "not important." And while Box 1 may contain valuable work such as immediate but worthwhile tasks and goal-oriented projects with tight deadlines, we will always turn to Box 2 as soon as they are done – simply because tasks in Box 2 are also "urgent" and therefore shout louder.

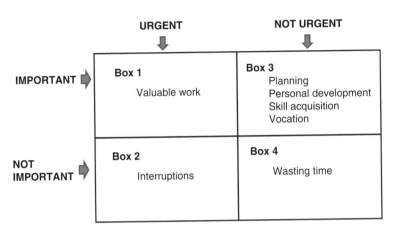

Figure 11.1 Stephen Covey's four activity boxes

Yet this is a disaster for our progress. Box 2, of urgent but unimportant tasks, is the box that knocks those with high fear of failure off course. Unable to prioritize, fearful of saying no, we try and balance Boxes 1 and 2 but have only the vaguest notion of what activities are important for goal achievement and what requires our focus simply to get someone off our back. And the two combined wipe out our potential for growth, which is nearly all stored in Box 3 – containing not urgent but nonetheless important tasks.

Box 2 deceives us into thinking we are making progress, but is in fact no more than the processing of interruptions such as emails, phone calls, meetings, enquiries from adjacent colleagues and other ultimately useless activities. Box 3, meanwhile, contains important future-oriented activities such as research, relationship-building, applications, skill-acquisition and planning.

Amazingly, Box 3 is the least loved of all the boxes, despite being the most important. Exhausted after a day working through Boxes 1 and 2, we flop into the escapist "not urgent, not important" activities of Box 4. This really is the time-wasters box – usually involving mind-numbing TV or internet surfing – although can

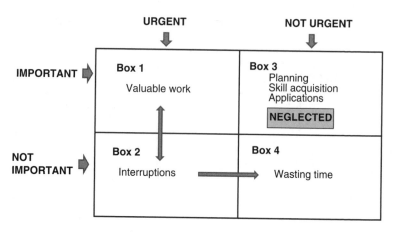

Figure 11.2 What happens

include some pleasant activities that could potentially be recategorized as "important," such as family time or exercise, once we are on top of time-and-task management.

Rethinking the notion of time

So how can we create the space to focus on Box 3? This can be difficult, but by focusing on our 10-year horizon and our thought-through strategy we should have achieved the mental realignment required to begin with Box 3 activities – using it as our starting grid to drive our every action. Where we used to start with Box 1, and fit in Box 3 if released long enough from the "urgent" stranglehold, we now use Box 3 to determine what counts as Box 1 (valuable) and Box 2 (interruption) – giving us the judgement to prioritize. Sure, this may overload Box 2 (with all our old work now judged as no more than an interruption), but at least we have become aware of that fact.

A second requirement is to rethink our notion of time.

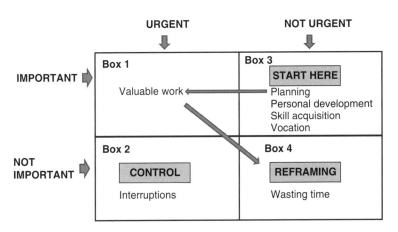

Figure 11.3 What should happen

"We may have leisure time, but no one has such a thing as free time," says corporate consultant and academic B. Eugene Griessman in *Time Tactics of Very Successful People* (1994). "You may be lying by the pool or attending a play, but that's not free time. All time has value."

Griessman states that you should develop a full appreciation of the value of time, if necessary allocating a theoretical monetary cost for each hour depending on what you think an hour of your time is worth. That said, the aim is not to be "crudely materialistic." It is to help you realize that – if you are in a meeting that's dragging on, or you are talking too frequently to your colleague – you understand the true cost *to you* of that meeting or conversation (or even that wasteful out-of-hours activity).

If necessary, says Griessman, you should keep a log of your daily ration of 24 hours (perhaps in your diary) so that you can analyze over a period where you have allocated your time, and its cost. Quickly it should become apparent where the efficiencies are to be had – what activities are in the unimportant boxes and should, therefore, be squeezed or eliminated.

Create a timetable

Yet Griessman's recommendations can seem complicated. Covey's simpler approach, meanwhile, takes us back to school – actually creating a school-style timetable with hourly slots from eight-til-eight and blocks for the evening. You should allocate each hour of the day for particular activities – importantly allowing you to schedule time for the vital Box 3 activities no matter what the pressures from Box 1 and 2.

The timetable uses all seven days and requires you to state your weekly and daily priorities and your weekly goals against your particular roles (e.g. father, husband, manager, future entrepreneur). And while you need to be realistic about time allocation for each task, you also need to be strict on yourself regarding the need to complete tasks within the allotted timeframe before moving on – not engaging in other activities until you have completed your tasks.

Yet even this can become unsustainable. Such an approach will work well for initially improving your time-management practices – as well as making you acutely aware of being bamboozled by Box 2 activities. But only the most swivel-eyed self-motivators will want to regiment their lives to the point where the kids are being dragged to badminton because that's what it says on the timetable. It is also an easy timetable to write but one less easy to follow because your energy and motivation levels are not always consistent. Slotting in two hours last thing on Friday afternoon for "ideas and creativity" may be pushing your luck with respect to motivation, for instance, although it may be just the time to discuss ideas in the pub with the rest of the team.

In *The Time Trap* MacKenzie suggests we understand our personal energy cycle before setting up our "ideal day" with respect to timetabling. And, certainly, we need some flexibility within the system, although what I notice when strictly pursuing Covey's timetable is that, if I follow it from Monday, such strong time-structuring means most of my Box 1 and 2 tasks are complete by

Wednesday, allowing me to focus on Box 3 items for Thursday and Friday (and on reframed Box 4 activities at the weekend).

Proactively managing interruptions

But what of those nasty Box 2 items, derailing our agendas? Of course, it's impossible to kill all interruptions – at least without making ourselves unpopular. Yet it may help to allot particular times for dealing with them – perhaps from nine-til-10 am and/or from five-til-six pm. It just might be the case that you can also politely and over time train those around you to respect those hours for "urgent" but not important interruptions.

Well you can at least try, although it may be helped by proactivity on your part – Box 2 interruptions are usually from a handful of the same individuals, so a quick call at 9 am – asking if they have all they need for the day because "I need to knuckle down on a major project and will be keen to minimize interruptions" – may just work if delivered in a style aimed at making their work seem valued and necessary (rather than the eye-rolling job-creation you may inwardly believe it to be).

Clearing roadblocks

Yet what if you can't even get this far – so cluttered is the path in front of you? This usually means there's a roadblock preventing you getting started. A roadblock so large, what's more, that you cannot see the road ahead because of it. In *Getting Things Done* (2001), executive coach David Allen accepts that your first job may be to create the sense of control and focus you need for the road ahead – perhaps clearing that major project or task by writing a list of everything you need to do to move that project forward.

This may be a struggle, although as long as you remain clear about the intention of making headway towards your goals, you should soon manage to navigate the obstacle. And even with the roadblock, Covey's timetable may help breathe some oxygen into your schedule – perhaps allowing an hour a day on Box 3 activities – even while in the thick of battle to overcome your roadblock.

In *The Power of an Hour* (2006), "business acceleration" consultant Dave Lakhani discusses the "critical power hour" that allows you to address such major roadblocks by working out what you need to change, what is the structure of the change, what solutions are possible, what are the next steps, and how you will reward ourselves once done. As the name of his book suggests, Lakhani divides life's tasks into hours that have a "fearsome focus" with a relaxing break at the end.

"While time may seem like the thing you need the most of," he says, "it turns out that isn't true. What you need is focus – a very specific kind of focus."

This complements Covey's timetable. And Lakhani's recommendations also chime with David Allen's advice that, when facing that initial roadblock, you first create a physical place that captures everything you need to get done – now, later or some time – into a logical and organized system, such as a ring-binder. Just maybe your roadblock is not as large as it seems, once you have properly assessed its proportions and how it might be navigated.

"Sharpening the saw"

One of my favourite tricks for unblocking "big-taskitis" is to buy some stationery. These are the tools of the organized person and, just as a mountaineer will spend hours looking at equipment for an expedition – seeing it as a thrilling precursor to the adventure ahead – so you should fall in love with the stationery store. Files, folders, wallets, organizers, in-trays, memo-pads: this is the equipment you need to climb your mountain and you should indulge yourself with new and shiny objects and arrange them lovingly around your desk.

You should also spend time arranging your desk. David Allen states that you should schedule a block of time dedicated to preparing your workstation – sourcing the necessary furniture, cabinets, intrays and electronic equipment, making sure it is arranged as you want it, is configured and primed to your needs, and is both efficient and pleasing to look at. Once done, you should admire it. It will be your cockpit for the journey ahead.

This is what Stephen Covey calls "sharpening the saw" – his seventh habit in fact. In *Seven Habits . . .* he offers a parable in which a man, struggling to fell a tree, is advised to sharpen the old rusty saw he is using.

"I don't have time to sharpen the saw, I'm too busy sawing," says the man, and struggles on inefficiently.

Just about every "success" writer agrees with this, even Abraham Lincoln.

"Give me six hours to chop down a tree and I will spend the first four sharpening the axe," is one of his attributed quotes.

Certainly, preparation is a key part of our drive for time-and-task efficiency, as are the right tools.

"Make your workplace work for you," says Griessman (1994), adding that you should spend money on the files and equipment you need to work efficiently and effectively.

And if memo-pads and files sound a bit "last century," perhaps they should. Sure Covey's timetable can be electronic, as can project documents. However, Allen's idea of a "collection bucket" for anything unfinished, so it can be "released from your mind" but still apparent as a "to do," needs to be physical in my view. My PC's hard-drive is full of electronic folders that have been created and then forgotten, yet every physical file that has ever been on my desk has been dealt with, no matter how far down the pile it sank or even if it was eventually consciously thrown away. The key thing is that it wasn't lost and forgotten.

"To do" lists and "checklists"

Such physicality is also required of your diary in my view – not least because it needs to be locatable for 10 years, which few electronic formats are (due to changing technologies) – and it is even true of reminders or "to do" lists. These can even be in your diary, although I'd rather not have my diary so visible – preferring instead those 6x4 inch lined cards where I list my tasks for the next few days, crossing them off when complete. The size of the card is important as I can only fit 12-or-so tasks on the list before having to start a new card. Sure, some tasks get backed up, and some cards need to have undone tasks transferred between them. Yet the simple process of transferring a task from one card to another reminds me of the task and helps me reassess it. The cards are then propped behind my keyboard and stare at me all day. Box 2 interruptions are simply given a line on the card and dealt with between five and six pm.

Importantly, Box 3 needs are given equal billing to Box 1. And any "manage the process" elements, such as a need to renew my passport, collect my suit from the dry cleaners or buy my wife's birthday present(s) also get a line, as well as a line through them once done.

"Learn to rely on checklists," recommends Griessman (1994), although he also states that these are not to be confused with "to do" lists (as described above). Checklists note the steps we must take to complete a task efficiently. For instance everything we need for a trip abroad is a checklist, everything I needed to do to allow me to focus on nothing but my speech – including quick calls to reception to request a late checkout – is a checklist.

Checklists are about efficiency, so order is also important. In *Getting Things Done*, David Allen states that there are five stages when dealing with workflow:

- *Collect* – create a (physical) file to capture everything that is on your to-do list.

- *Process* – work out how to deal with each item. Is it for now or after another item? What needs doing? Is it perhaps for "reference only" or "research further" or "contact now?"
- *Organize* – create a system (perhaps a checklist) that reflects your decisions regarding priority and the actionable plans you have for each item.
- *Do* – undertake the actionables. Allen recommends one of four criteria for making sure you are in the best place for action. Context (which location – home, work?), time (how long do you need and have you timetabled that block?), energy (can you see this through to completion?), and priority (is this the "now" task, or is there something else more pressing – though beware the Box 2 bully? If not now, when?).
- *Review* – use Covey's timetable to slot weekly review moments for the file – going back to "process."

Griessman would perhaps add "get it done now" to Allen's list. He states that it is damaging to start a project, put it away, and then start again – spending time wondering "where was I?" Some projects cannot be finished in one go but many can and should. Also, you should stop midway only after giving yourself clear written instructions about what comes next once you restart.

Griessman also suggests that you "ask yourself, 'is there an easier way to do this?'"

"Looking for the easy way out can be the smartest thing you can do," he says. "Don't confuse 'busyness' with efficiency."

Deal with the worst thing first

A final Griessman tip worth adopting is to deal with unpleasant situations first. Immediately tackling the tasks that give us least comfort can make them more bearable. Indeed, these tasks are often the very roadblocks that are obscuring the way ahead.

Brian Tracy (of *Goals!* fame) writes something similar in *Eat That Frog* (2004), although uses more descriptive language – suggesting that if you "eat a live frog each morning" you will have already experienced the worst thing that will happen to you that day. He says you should find the live frogs that are hidden on your to-do list or checklists and tackle them first – learning to "snack on those difficult problems."

Of course by frogs Tracy means the largest and/or most important and/or most difficult task facing you on your path towards progress.

"The ability to concentrate single-mindedly on your most important task, to do it well and to finish it completely, is the key to great success," says Tracy – suggesting that the frogs are a "high-protein diet" that will give you the right physique for dealing with all the other tasks.

Prioritization and efficiency

This feeds into Tracy's thinking on prioritization – offering a tip that can easily be added to your to-do list or checklist or to Covey's timetable. He calls it the "ABCs of Success" although also adds D and E. His suggestion is that you categorize your to-do list with an ABCD or E:

- An "A" task is one that you must complete as soon as possible or "face serious consequences,"
- "B" items are important tasks that carry "mild consequences,"
- "C" tasks are nice to do but with "no consequences,"
- "D" tasks can be delegated (see Part Four), and
- "E" tasks should be eliminated.

Of course, the stressed person may be tempted to load their tasks with "A" and "B" labels, which Tracy says is fine – "simply number them sequentially . . . A-1, A-2, A-3 and so forth."

I also think it important to be opportunistic when it comes to efficiency. Helped by my RAS, I am always on the lookout for a chance to quickly fulfil a need. Queueless cashpoints always attract my eye, for instance, and I never pass the stationery store without it occurring to me that this may be a good moment to stock up.

Yet this can go beyond small tasks. Grabbing a coffee or a sandwich is a great opportunity to discuss a major project with a colleague; travel to meetings offers a strong chance to read boring documents that have to be digested (often called "airplane reading" in the US) or practise presentational skills with a colleague; and commuting offers us an excellent opportunity to undertake Box 3 tasks such as acquiring knowledge and research.

Endeavour is the key

Does all this sound a bit manic? Perhaps it should. In his groundbreaking book *Outliers* (2008), renowned business author Malcolm Gladwell focuses on what turns ordinary mortals into outstanding achievers. One clear trait is endeavour. In tracking potential professional musicians, he states that researchers noticed a pattern between the hours of practice and the level of achievement. Strong amateurs put in around 2000 hours by adulthood while teachers put in around 4000. Professionals, however, put in around 8000 hours and the elite 10,000.

"Virtually every success story . . . involves someone or some group working harder than their peers," was Gladwell's conclusion.

Hard work matters. No one else will achieve your goals on your behalf. But does that mean you are never off duty, never relaxed? All this activity can make you feel and appear hyper, which can irritate those around you and lead to nervous exhaustion. Your aim here is not to alienate people who may now seem to you disinterested, disorganized and, frankly, in the slow lane. You are simply trying to make progress towards *your* goals by producing better results. You must realize that this will take time and may not always involve smooth progress, so you may need to inject some wind-down time within your schedule if you are not to burn out. And you must also realize that you remain connected to others – especially significant others – and shouldn't alienate them through your potentially over-zealous words and actions.

This means you should reframe those Box 4 "not urgent and not important" tasks. If they are the moments you reconnect with friends and family – making sure you are carrying them with you on your journey – then Box 4 has its place. If Box 4 tasks are also the moments you can recharge your batteries with exercise, disconnected stimulation or relaxation then they definitely have their place. And if they are, crucially, the moments you reflect on the tiny self-confirming steps you are taking each day then they are valuable indeed.

Case Study 11 – Churchill the efficiency guru

Britain's war leader Winston Churchill was known for his courage and rhetorical flair. He is less well known, however, for his tremendous abilities as an organizer, although it was the key to his success.

At the start of each day Churchill wrote a note "Action of the Day," in order to ensure that something important was achieved. And despite appearances, his day was well structured. He spent most mornings lying in bed dictating to secretaries (who even had to follow him into the bathroom). While portrayed as an eccentricity, it was in fact a ruse for avoiding (Box 2) meetings in those crucial morning hours when his mind was most fertile.

Certainly, Churchill was a man who could order his desk and his mind for efficiency. But it didn't stop there. He even developed his trademark wartime boiler-suit as part of a time-saving personal preparation process to free up vital minutes for more work. He was thrilled by industrial process and saw that it could be adopted in all areas, including his writing, which followed the three Ds: documents, dictation and drafts (i.e. source material, drafting and editing).

He was also good at getting on top of any bureaucracy. He wouldn't fight it. He'd understand it – working out how decisions were made and who were the key players. He also had a strong eye for delegation (see Part Four). Having set a very clear objective – total victory – and having had his say with respect to the strategy (total war), he'd learnt from his mistakes in WWI and never interfered once the orders were given – he simply found the most talented people he could for the task and gave them complete operational control (unlike Hitler, whose constant meddling left his generals weak and fearful).

And despite working 16-hour days, Churchill usually slept soundly – not least because, when the occasion allowed, he could completely switch off (which certainly sets him apart from the usual High-FF trait of obsessing about our problems). With typical enthusiasm and competitiveness he became an expert bricklayer (and sought membership of the bricklayers' union) and a strong painter (anonymously judged as a professional-standard landscape artist). In later years his writing output was also prolific.

But Churchill never forgot his objective (in both war and peace) – a focus that gave him strong judgement, the appearance of great confidence in the face of adversity and a motto that every High-FF should immediately adopt: KBO ("keep buggering on").

What's Stopping You? *Efficiency is not a skill or craft, it is a process anyone can adopt. You need to organize all your activities – scheduling your time correctly and setting yourself up for effective execution. Roadblocks, interruptions and time-wasting can all be dealt with to prevent them from halting your progress.*

PART FOUR
People

12

SELF-ESTEEM

We can develop strategies and execute tactics all we like. Sooner or later we are going to have to tackle people – probably the most challenging aspect of any recovery programme for those with high fear of failure.

"Fully 85 per cent of your success in life is going to be determined by your social skills," says Brian Tracy in *Maximum Achievement* (1993), "by your ability to interact positively and effectively with others and to get them to cooperate with you in helping you to achieve your goals."

Certainly, this is by far the most difficult chapter for me to write. Over the years my High-FF behaviour has destroyed more business and office relationships, more friendships and more romantic involvements than I dare to remember. I have been truly dreadful when it comes to my dealings with my fellow human beings: hurtful, angry, destructive and self-centred. And that's just with the people who were on my side. Out of fear, I suspect I have behaved rather better to those who did not have my best interests at heart.

Throughout my life I have nursed a burning sense of injustice – sometimes treating people appallingly because of an overly sensitized perception of prejudice against me, even from friends. I have jumped to every wrong conclusion, assumed every slight intended,absorbed every insult – meant or otherwise. I have also reacted angrily in defence on so many occasions that I have problems recalling any past period without immediately remembering some reactive episode I wish I could forget.

Yet High-FF reactivity goes way beyond angry responses. Poor reactions to social or people situations can equally encompass hurt, withdrawal and passivity, in which we fail to stand up for ourselves, or bitchiness and criticism, in which we seek revenge for perceived slights through backstabbing or passive aggressive behaviour such as being obstructive.

People skills are vital

Indeed, of all the failings of those with a high fear of failure, it is our dealings with people that most disable us. Surveys in the US have concluded that up to 95 per cent of men and women "let go" from their job over a 10-year period were fired due to poor social skills rather than lack of competence.

No matter how well you strategize to meet your objectives, therefore, if you fail to improve your people skills you will fail to make progress in your life. We cannot avoid people in the pursuit of our goals. In many respects, people *are* the goal as well as the means of achieving them. Yet they are also our greatest barrier. Without people skills we are illiterate in a land of words, innumerate in a land of numbers. We are deaf in a room filled with sound.

Those neural hijackings that act as the internal assassins of our objectivity are almost always triggered by someone else's words or actions, and our interpretations of the intentions behind them. Yet when dealing with people the depersonalization we should employ to help overcome such hijackings seems impossible. If somebody insults me – perceived or otherwise – it's not *Me Inc.* that's being insulted. It's me.

Low self-esteem – the distorting mirror

As a recovering High-FF, however, it is important to recognize that much of the alienation we have felt has not only been conceived and perceived in our own heads, it has been self-fulfilling and therefore self-inflicted. Sure hateful people exist (though they are mostly fellow High-FFs). But the person that really hates you – to the core of your being – that really doesn't have your best interests at heart, is you.

This is an awful and depressing realization. Yet – like taking responsibility – it is also a liberating thought. If you are your own worst enemy then you are the person that can exorcize the demon within that is destroying not only your life chances, but your friend-ships, relationships, partnerships and leaderships. That demon has got to go – and you are the only person that can throw him or her out.

The key issue here – the distorting mirror that generates the problems – is low self-esteem. As stated in Part One, not everyone with high fear of failure suffers from low self-esteem, although most do to either a lesser of greater extent (usually greater). And there is a direct relationship between self-esteem and our ability to get along with others.

"The more you like and respect yourself," says Tracy, "the more you like and respect others. The more you consider yourself to be a valuable and worthwhile person, the more you consider others to be valuable and worthwhile as well. The more you accept your-self just as you are, the more you accept others just as they are."

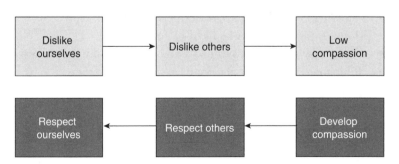

Figure 12.1 Reversing the flow of low self-esteem

And clearly this has a direct impact upon our ability to utilize the power of people to achieve our goals.

"Men and women with low self-esteem can only get along with a few people, and then not for very long," says Tracy. "Their low self-regard manifests itself in anger, impatience, criticism, bad-mouthing and arguments with the people around them."

As someone with low self-esteem this strikes home with painful clarity. We assume people do not like us as we dislike ourselves. This leads us not to like others, making their return of the feeling inevitable. Once again we are in a self-fulfilling and destructive vortex with the dizzying addition that, according to Tracy, this is the single most important reason why so many people fail to meet their objectives.

Deconstructing low self-esteem

In *Boost Your Self-Esteem*, John Caunt states that self-esteem issues present themselves in different ways, just about all of which are familiar to me. These include (with a few added thoughts of my own):

- Resenting others' success.
- Feeling like a failure.
- Focusing on the negative in any situation.
- Allowing even "constructive" criticism to derail us.
- Doing things purely to be liked or for approval.
- Comparing ourselves continually and detrimentally with others.
- Taking *everything* too personally.
- Giving in to others' desires.
- Changing or arresting behaviour for fear of looking foolish.
- Striving for perfection and being angry at not meeting unrealistic expectations.
- Worrying excessively, but avoiding seeking help.
- Feeling out of control, even panicking.

- Bullying and taking advantage of others.
- Putting ourselves and others down – publicly.
- Withdrawing from or avoiding social situations.
- Becoming aggressive, or even overly passive.
- Being boastful.
- Indulging in exaggeration if not downright lying in order to make ourselves more "interesting."

The persistence of such feelings – despite my strong growth thanks to the likes of Covey and Robbins *et al* – landed me back in the shrink's chair a year or so after my NHS counselling, determined to rid myself of the plagues of paranoia, fear, anger and low self-esteem that have conspired to make my entire life seem like a string of wrecked personal encounters.

Such appalling and disabling traits are, of course, developed from negative experiences in childhood. I was aware of what caused my own self-esteem issues, although further sessions with the psychoanalyst surprised me with respect to how they manifested themselves in my relationships. As a child, I knew I had a poor relationship with my father but hadn't realized I had subconsciously blamed my mother for this and therefore developed a resentment and irritation with the very person that had loved me the most. I also feared and resented the power of my sister – the apple of my father's eye.

Even writing this is painful but there it is: fear of rejection from the people whose love I sought while rejecting those who loved me unconditionally. Meanwhile, with peers: distrust, frustration, envy, paranoia. I didn't stand a chance of being able to develop strong social or people skills – I was far too busy throwing affection at those that didn't deserve it while collecting and then rejecting the commitment of those that did. As for peers, how could I be a suitable colleague or partner when, through mistrust and jealousy, I misinterpreted their every move?

As stated, self-esteem issues can have a profound impact on our ability to make progress in the workplace. We may be stymied by our inner beliefs and perceptions, to the point where we develop coping mechanisms to avoid pain, such as rejecting ourselves before others are allowed to. Perhaps we don't put ourselves forward for promotion – convincing ourselves it would be the wrong move. Or we adopt the persona of the office clown or the unthreatening (perhaps even withdrawn) "nice guy" that's happier among the troops than the officers. And we avoid confrontation because we cannot trust either our internal or external responses.

At least, those are the better responses. We could become the brooding back-stabber, the angry shouter (that was me) or the scheming Machiavellian. All are the typical traits of those with low self-esteem. And all are a disaster.

The fight back

So is there anything we can do? Of course. We can fight back, although we must remember the battle is internal. We have already spent our lives externalizing the battle with respect to dealing with people (even if just through withdrawal or submission). Now we must internalize it – turning the fire on the enemy within.

As I have stated before, there is no magic formula that can cure us, of either high fear of failure or low self-esteem. Our insecurities are not going to be wished (or self-hypnotized or acupunctured) away. Our default position is to undermine our self-belief and so encourage failure. Yet we can take small and progressive steps that help us develop better external responses, especially when it comes to dealing with people. We have been incorrectly wired to give a false reading on the intentions of others so that we interpret their actions wrongly and react inappropriately: defensiveness and anger at one end, shyness and withdrawal at the other – with us potentially flipping between these extremes.

Yet we must always remember that we are probably wrong. Did that person insult me, or dismiss me, or blank me? Maybe, but why assume so? If we assume it probably came out badly and they meant something more supportive or were distracted (as in the CBT example mentioned in Part One) then the result will almost certainly be better than if we assume the insult. This assumption may not be your first response, but can you make it your second? And can you make it your second response quickly – so quickly that you manage to externally suppress your first response? In time, hopefully, yes.

Judged by intentions, not actions

Like most people, I want to be judged on my intentions, not my actions, which may be misinterpreted for any number of reasons. So how can I deny this right to others? We must seek their intentions, not judge their actions.

If someone is brandishing a knife or gun in front of us it may be right to assume their intentions are aggressive. But there are thankfully few situations where this happens. And unlike guns or knives, words and body-language are open to wild misinterpretation. By assuming a better, kinder, interpretation – however hard this is to achieve – us are making it easier to respond appropriately.

In fact, the harder it is to perceive of a kinder interpretation the more it is in your advantage to seek and assume one. Let's go back to the man brandishing the knife or gun. This is a pretty clear act of aggression, most would agree. Yet look behind the weapon at the man and he may perceive *you* as the aggressor. He may be protecting a child or be expecting an attack from someone else, or he may have snapped at the series of negative events that led him to this awful point. He may even be drug-addled and therefore not in control of his perceptions or responses. So, while we need to deal with the threat, looking behind it may also generate a more disarming response from us.

See the best in others

Seeing the best in people is incredibly difficult. Yet it is absolutely in your advantage to do so. If the gunman's actions are hostile you are going to take the bullet no matter what. But if they are defensive then your hostility is going to escalate the situation to the point when he feels so threatened he'll shoot in apparent self-defence.

Yet what if we are totally wrong and our harshest interpretation is correct?

So what? By forcing ourselves to assume a kinder interpretation of their intentions – we misheard, they didn't realize what they were saying, they were very stressed, we have given them the wrong signals and made them defensive – we are neutralizing the impact their insult/slight will have on us. In fact, as with Eleanor Roosevelt's famous quote – "No one can make you feel inferior without your *consent*" – we are saying it has no impact. This throws the insult back to them. They have thrown a bomb but it didn't go off – *how embarrassing!*

This is absolutely on-the-money when it comes to my issues with anger. Countless times I have over-reacted to a perceived insult and the fallout from the insult has been about *my* response rather than *their* insult – all adding to my burning sense of injustice. But I have learnt that – painful is this may seem – assuming a kinder intention on their part is the *only* way of developing a better response from me.

Spreading positivity

And assuming a kinder intention (however forced it feels at first) has further benefits. It starts to undermine the other props of your low self-esteem. By developing positivity about something – anything – it can spread elsewhere, even to you. In *Boost Your Self-Esteem* John Caunt suggests we practise techniques that reframe the information we feed our brain, helping create more positive attitudes and opinions, which – over time and with positive and reinforcing steps – help build our self-esteem, or at least disrupt the thought process that leads to our default low self-esteem assumptions.

These include (again, with some thoughts of my own):

- *Recognize your positive qualities.* This is one for the diary – listing all the good qualities about you. These are the qualities to focus on, not those you perceive as negative.
- *Indulge in positive self-talk.* Pay attention to what you say to yourself. Instead of self-harming language you must use positive or forgiving language. That monkey has no monopoly on your inner thoughts – it *can* and should be countered.
- *Question your thoughts and opinions.* Not just your views on others. You need to challenge your views on yourself – they are likely to be irrational and probably wrong. As Anthony Robbins says, there is no such thing as truth – only perception.
- *Associate with positive people.* Low-self-esteemers can find themselves in a negative club, especially in the office. Perhaps it is the smokers' coterie or the moaning canteen gang. Pull away from them, or – even better – start using positive language when with them (although avoid becoming the preaching motivational convert – remember, it is only *your* behaviour you are trying to change).
- *Acknowledge achievements.* You should keep a list (in the obvious place) of what you have achieved – however small. These are the building blocks of future achievement.
- *Accept what you cannot change.* Learn to accept what you cannot change (as with Covey's Circle of Concern). This may be more than just the weather but there is little about your situation that you cannot change with good planning and strong endeavour. Yet you need to be realistic and embrace the unchangeable, and that includes the past.
- *Detach yourself.* Yoga, sports, fiction, biographies – you must find something positive that takes you somewhere else, avoiding

quick-fix diversions such as alcohol or drugs that will simply compound your negative feelings once they wear off.

- *Develop self-reliance.* You should not seek constant approval. Instead, you should trust your skills and be pleased with yourself without external affirmation. Don't seek to impress others – just be inwardly content with the small steps you are taking in the right direction.

- *Stop comparing yourself to others.* You are being unfair to yourself – we are all unique. You should not ape others but develop your singular qualities, although some mild NLP-style modelling of effective behaviour in others may help undermine your destructive behaviours (such as defensiveness in conversation). But don't *ever* wish to be someone else, not least because it is impossible, so such a desire will simply add to your frustration.

- *Learn to laugh at yourself.* You should laugh at your flaws – we all have them.

- *Accept praise.* Be graceful, but don't deflect it. You deserve it, though should not seek to expand it or reinforce it yourself. Just say "thank you."

- *Focus on the lessons.* From both your successes and your failures, there are lessons to be learnt. You should seek them out and focus on those when you recall past errors, or even current successes.

- *Learn to say "no."* You should not be a people pleaser, just because you seek their approval. Your every action should be judged against your long-term goals and thought-through strategy, although keeping people onside will always be useful when pursuing your objectives.

Of course, the above points are easily written. Turning our self-harming and deeply held assumptions into positives can feel like an impossible task, especially with that monkey offering negative feedback. Yet it is worth the effort and, in fact, can provide quick confirmation that we are heading in the right direction. Simply by reversing the direction we are travelling, we are immediately making headway towards our goals. And by noting that every small step leads to the next step – that every brick laid is the platform for the next brick – we can slowly, over time, get beyond the highest barrier of all: our own negative self-view.

Case study 12 – The fat kid

I was amazed when Helen told me she'd been bullied as a child for being fat. Now a mother in her 40s she looked positively spindly as she stood up to greet me in the Soho café we'd arranged for a light lunch.

"It's impacted everything I've ever done," she said, "including how much I eat to this day."

The fat may be long gone, but the trauma of being the taunted and excluded fat kid had never left her, not least because, chief amongst the bullies, had been her own mother.

"I was definitely publicly humiliated," she confessed. "Mum would openly talk about *her* problem with *my* weight in front of me: to relations, friends, even acquaintances in the street. 'Why did I have to have the fat kid?' she used to ask."

"I just closed up," said Helen. "At school I was the last one picked for teams and was never in the gang – instead becoming a bit of a swot."

Her withdrawal also had a major impact on her youth and adulthood.

"I was painfully shy – not wanting to draw attention to myself," she said. "This even had an impact at university. Sure, I now had friends, but I had no idea how to behave in social situations. For instance, on rowdy nights out my behaviour would be that much worse than others because I'd developed no social skills when younger."

Helen went into the graduate scheme of a large organization but failed to make an impression.

"I never put myself forward for promotion," she said. "I was just going through the motions, completely inward, private and submissive – surrendering before any challenge. I assumed everyone knew more than me and was better than me."

After being made redundant (her quiet diligence meant she'd made little impression on the seniors) she used the career gap to do some belated travelling, some thinking and some effective skill-acquisition – enrolling on one of Richard Bandler's NLP programmes.

Here she learnt some techniques for projecting more effective body language and speech.

"It taught me where I was going wrong with people," she said.

It was also where she met her future husband, the product of which has channelled her new energies.

"No, I'm not going to end up a hedge fund manager or supervisor of scores of people," she said. "But I do think I've got something to say with respect to using NLP for natural childbirth."

And the birth of her child – by "hypnobirthing" techniques – had helped develop her true values, which she now wants to convert into a career helping other mothers through the "potentially terrifying" experience of first-time birthing.

What's Stopping You? *"No one can make you feel inferior without your consent," so you should focus on reframing the thoughts and traits that undermine your self-esteem. Thinking more positively of those around you is an important building block for improving your own self-view.*

13

DEALING WITH THE BOSS

Developing people skills is vital whether you are dealing with your boss, your peers and colleagues, your potential customers, or your employees. As someone with fear of failure trying to make progress in your career, however, the person most likely to loom largest is your boss.

There's no getting away from it – working for a bad boss is hell. A bad boss can obsess, oppress and depress us – reducing a potentially enjoyable job to a confidence-sapping imprisonment. Many people alter course in their careers, often with disastrous results, simply to escape a bad boss. My decision to become an entrepreneur, for instance, was majorly influenced by some appalling experiences in this respect (made far worse, no doubt, by the distorting mirror of my own insecurities).

Yet if you are convinced a key barrier for your progress is your current line manager you are far from alone. According to one study – quoted in *Dealing with the Boss from Hell* (2005) by leadership consultant Shaun Belding – around 75 per cent of 1800 Australian workers surveyed stated they were unhappy with their managers, and US studies have produced similar findings.

And the reality, according to Belding, is that you have few remedies. Any direct confrontation is unlikely to produce positive results and could end up a "career limiting move" – jeopardizing rather than enhancing your progress.

"The hardest part of having a boss from hell is that very few resources are available to you for dealing with him or her," says Belding, so "don't shoot yourself in the foot" by publicly embarrassing, threatening or openly challenging your boss, he cautions.

Belding recommends that you wait before you act, you control your impulses and that you look beyond the immediate future towards the long-term consequences of your actions. Yet you can also develop some strong strategies and tactics aimed at not allowing a bad boss to derail your career.

Three types of bad boss

Belding states that bad bosses usually fall into one of three types – aggressive, passive or controlling – all of which throw up significant problems for less confident people. Yet, believe it or not, all also provide opportunities for progress. The aggressive boss can seem the most immediately debilitating. However, in most modern companies bullying behaviour such as shouting or intimidation is now viewed as unacceptable. So – while such behaviour is upsetting and potentially terrifying – the aggressive boss is, in my view, laying the foundations of his or her own demise.

Aggressive bosses are usually weak – often High-FFs themselves – and are therefore reasonably easy to manage once you realize this. Their behaviour is also usually well known, meaning that your suffering has probably been noticed further up the organization, although they may choose not to act. Deal well with the aggressive boss, and you will have acquired some significant and transferable people skills that will put you in a strong position no matter what your future.

Passive bosses also present opportunities. According to Belding, such bosses are usually shy and avoid decisions, conflicts, risks and strong individuals. They may be frustrating and inspire only contempt but they are also less likely to present a major barrier to your progress. In fact, in my opinion they are worth befriending and aiding. If you support their seniority, rather than undermine it, you are likely to have recruited perhaps your most significant ally towards your own goal achievement. Again, their weakness is unlikely to have gone unnoticed by their own reports, meaning that your assistance and support will also be noticed, although, again, this may not be obvious.

The Pisstaker's Charter

This brings me to the most difficult of all boss-related situations – dealing with someone trying to control or manipulate you, perhaps (in fact probably) leveraging off your insecurities in an attempt to steer the situation to their advantage. While aggressive or insulting bosses are often fellow High-FFs and therefore reasonably transparent in their goals, the manipulators have achievement motivation coursing through their veins and are far more difficult to read. They have also noticed your insecurities and are taking advantage.

I call this the *Pisstaker's Charter* – the notion that confident people can so effectively take advantage of under-confident people that we end up doing their bidding for them – with them even feigning surprise and hurt when we finally snap and resist. In fact, their surprise can be genuine, so used are they to getting the better of us by manipulating our insecurities, and so poor have we been at projecting our own needs.

My own experience here is a painful one – in fact, probably the most painful of my working life. The details need to remain obscure but such was the manipulation I experienced from one line manager that I felt was taking advantage of my low confidence that I was forced to fight back. Certainly I felt I was being used in ways that compromised my position, first as a screen for his unethical behaviour and later as the person being blamed for its consequences.

Eventually, my career became so threatened by his actions that I had to report him. News came to me that the senior management were contemplating firing *me* with respect to *my* conduct (as reported by him) despite the fact it was, in my view, clearly *his* behaviour causing the problems. Given this, I felt I had no choice but to act. I spoke of my suspicions to the senior management and, within a few (agonizing) months, he was gone.

Developing better responses

My actions resulted in someone losing their job and I have lived with the guilt ever since. And if that sounds odd given the circumstances, I see it as a sign of my growth that I can now see that it was my poor handling of the episode that allowed it to escalate. And it was my insecurities that caused it to develop in the first place. The situation was my fault, not his.

Here's what I could have done differently:

- *I could have been less emotional.* My overly emotional responses when the problems developed weakened my position – especially with the senior management – and lost me the respect of colleagues and allies. Of course, it is difficult for insecure people to simply switch off their emotions – especially when we feel an injustice is being perpetrated – but it is possible. Taking time to rationalize the situation, perhaps by writing notes (in the obvious place), would have been one way. Another would have been through knowing *all* the facts.

- *I could have been on top of the details.* Indeed, the key issues came down to facts and figures, so there was no need for my overly emotional responses when a forensic look at the details would have provided the answers. I should have been like Lieutenant Columbo after a murder, sifting through the evidence line by line. I could have calmly kept on asking questions, and – if blocked – I could have suggested a third party gets involved, perhaps one of the senior managers. In truth I had a very poor handle on the details, and it was this as much as my insecurities that gave him room for manoeuvre. In fact, some of the more minor problems *were* my fault, which gave me an inner sense of guilt and him all the space he needed to make hay. In any manipulative situation, the facts are sacred: get to the bottom of them (even if some of them highlight painful truths). And we also need to operate at the most professional level possible.

- *I could have levelled with him.* Actually, I tried this but received a dead-eyed denial, forcing me to back off. But that's because he was emotionally stronger than me. If I'd said it straight: "if this doesn't stop I'll report you" I may have got through. Sure, this may have wrecked our relationship and further endangered me, but the relationship was dead the moment his behaviour threatened my career. Fear, of course (and ignorance of the details), stopped me – so I went behind his back, which was a painful and bloody process that damaged my reputation.

- *Or I could have developed a kinder view.* This is the ultimate strategy, although one impossible to achieve when fighting High-FF neural hijackings at every turn. Kindness? To such manipulative swine? Absolutely. Our aim should not be to become like them. Not only is this impossible – we are High-FFs with our default responses hardwired into us – it is also undesirable. Their behaviour towards others is not to be emulated. Instead, we must seek an alternative route through understanding and kindness.

One excellent book dealing with this conundrum is Richard Carlson's rather homely *Don't Sweat the Small Stuff* (1988). Spending most of its pages addressing people problems, the book divides into seemingly unconnected 300-word (or so) tips for dealing with both big themes and small irritations. Yet the beauty of the book is that these sometimes twee recommendations build into a totally new approach – taking on some of life's greatest barriers.

Perhaps the most important of Carlson's tips for dealing with people is to "develop your compassion." Just as we did with the gunman in the previous chapter, we must put ourselves in their shoes in order to formulate our best response. Even our manipulative boss will face pressures perhaps forcing him or her to behave in a particular way.

In my own case, my rival had found himself in an excruciating personal situation that was clearly having an impact on his behaviour. Even at the time I could see the agonies he faced but showed no empathy because, in my view, he was behaving badly towards me. I felt he was making *me* pay the price for *his* circumstances, which led me to condemn him as morally selfish – itself a ridiculous notion (since when was I so pure I could affect moral outrage?).

Understand their weaknesses

If you recognize the difficulties others face, you can immediately develop sympathy for them, which – if you are freer than them of such pressures – liberates your responses. You have also garnered your most important piece of intelligence about this person: their weakness. Sun Tze would be proud, although he would also implore you to act in your long-term interest, which may not involve an instant full-frontal attack.

But what if you are convinced your tormentor has no pressures – that he or she leads a gilded existence? Then you simply haven't looked hard enough, largely because your RAS has been incorrectly tuned. Obsessed by their impact on you, you haven't noticed the manipulator as a person – trying to achieve his or her goals and relieve his or her agonies.

Once you spot these you are immediately looking them in the eye as an equal. In fact, you are more than equals as your behaviour is somewhat better than theirs. You understand them and have compassion for their situation. They think they understand you but are forced to behave poorly due to the pressures upon them.

Another relevant Carlson homily states that we should "see the innocence" in the actions of others. People are people, and "other people do weird things," is Carlson's view. Yet if we are the ones becoming upset by it, we are the ones that need to change or at least "look beyond it."

Of course, there is a danger in this – that we develop the "you're the insecure one" mentality of the motivational converts. This would be a disaster in my opinion. It is unsustainable and easily defeated because it isn't true. *We are the insecure ones*. We are simply trying to develop better responses when our insecurities are triggered.

Developing win–win situations

And once we have true empathy with our tormentors they are no longer our tormentors. At this point we can fight back and win. And if this sounds contradictory, given the empathy we have developed, then that's because we mostly view winning as a zero-sum game. We are taught "I win, you lose" situations from an early age. Certainly, that's how our manipulator would view it. But it doesn't have to be that way. We can seek a win–win.

Developing win–win solutions is one of Stephen Covey's seven habits. Not only are they preferable, they are the *only* sustainable way for a recovering High-FF to make progress. We are not good at win–lose battles so we should avoid them – instead fighting battles that create advantages for everyone involved.

So by understanding our manipulator we have created a relationship of equals. We can now offer help before it is asked, seek ways for them to achieve their victories, align ourselves with their goals. And then ask the same of them. They'll have little choice but to accept – not least because, deep down, they will also view themselves as good people.

And if this sounds naïve, that our tormentors will simply view our generosity as a weakness and gobble up the advantage – using it as a chance to manipulate us further – then so be it. We will be in a better place mentally than if we nurse grievances and battle back, either openly or through passive aggressive obstruction.

Remember, you have your long-term goals in place and are executing an effective strategy for achieving them. So this is no more than a temporary roadblock, however large it feels. Treat it as one of Tracy's frogs and it'll straighten out your thinking, as well as create the right imagery for putting the issue into perspective.

Case Study 13 – The bullying boss

I'd known Graeme for many years and been told the story of his first boss on several occasions, although I had only recently heard the facts that were to change his perspective on the situation.

Graeme had worked at a weekly magazine for an editor well known for a manner that would, these days, be considered bullying. And when Graeme ventured a disagreement with his boss in an editorial meeting, his career began to slide. At first, the editor's response had been no more than sarcasm in the office – mild public humiliation delivered as a not-so-funny joke. But, over time, the editor's aggression hardened into public insults, often about Graeme's Scottish roots, or speech foibles, or – most upsetting for Graeme – his work (which had previously been viewed positively).

Soon, Graeme was taking the blame for any mishap the team experienced and it became clear that the editor's unkindness had a darker purpose – to get Graeme out.

"One morning I was taken to a meeting room and sacked," said Graeme. "I'd done nothing wrong – my work was some of the best on the magazine. And I felt it all went back to this one disagreement with the editor, which I'd thought was no more than an open discussion about ideas."

Graeme's confidence was hugely affected – killing much of the creativity that had got him noticed and driven his career. And he struggled to find alternative employment.

"I guess my confidence had always been fragile," he said. "But I now felt like a complete loser."

Yet there was more to the story than meets the eye. The editor's actions were being dictated by pressure from above. The publishers were threatening to close the title, and in fact did so within months of Graeme's sacking. In an effort to save the magazine the editor had been forced to reduce the headcount, but had no experience how to go about choosing which person to fire from his team – all of whom he considered excellent.

And his clumsiness – cruelty even – was further explained by a fact Graeme only uncovered when bumping into a former colleague years later. The editor's father had been diagnosed with cancer during this hellish period, an event that had changed his behaviour towards everyone.

"I was told that he started being horrible to all the team," said Graeme. "I guess he just couldn't cope with the shock – as well as the stress of the failing magazine – and he just hit out."

What's Stopping You? *Bad bosses are usually aggressive, passive or controlling. All are problematic but all can provide opportunities for you to develop strong people skills. Dealing with a manipulative boss is incredibly difficult, but one way is to "develop your compassion" – they too will face pressures that are dictating their behaviour and you will be in a better place mentally if you can empathize.*

14

PROGRESS AS AN EMPLOYEE

Goal achievement within a large organization immediately presents difficulties for those with a high fear of failure that go way beyond enduring a bad boss. In many ways dealing with a bad boss is preferable to having no ready excuse for our lack of progress. Without such barriers, who or what do we blame as we watch those with high achievement motivation rise to the top?

We blame ourselves, of course, because High-FFs are capable of developing strong techniques for making progress within a large (or not so large) organization. If you stop listening to the monkey on your back and instead start looking at the people you work with and the organization you work for – and start aligning yourself with their needs – then headway is assured or, at the very least, you are in the right frame of mind to make progress, or move to an organization where progress is possible.

According to psychotherapist Barton Goldsmith in *Emotional Fitness at Work* (2009), high achievers have many traits in common, including confidence in their abilities and a trust in their instincts. Lifelong students, they are voracious readers pursuing knowledge in diverse areas. They tend to research answers to problems, asking many questions. And they are good at delegation – surrounding themselves with bright, energetic, talented peers, says Goldsmith. Finally, they live their lives according to their inner moral compass: defining, setting and achieving realistic goals.

The last part has been dealt with and the first part – regarding confidence and trust in your instincts – will come with time and the progress possible when small victories start to add up. But what about being lifelong students and researching answers to problems? This may well be an area the High-FF has neglected, perhaps because we perceive that the organization we work for is not deserving of our intellectual commitment.

This may be true, which means we should find an organization that is. Indeed, one of the first decisions you have to make when starting on the road to goal achievement is whether you are in the right organization. Are you standing at the bottom of the right ladder, as Stephen Covey would put it? If your conclusion is that you are on the wrong ladder, then your early Box 3 research should be focused on finding the right organization as well as on calculating how to get in the door.

Understand the organization

But what if you *are* in the right place? Then your research should be on that organization. What's stopping you from understanding the history and current structure of the company or organization you work for? It is almost certainly all available to read. You should be interested in the chief executive and the other senior managers – wanting to know their backgrounds and experiences. Not only will it make fascinating reading – as anything immediately relevant to us should – it offers a strong insight into where the organization has come from and where it is heading.

However, you should widen your interest from just the organization. What about your sector? Every industry sector has its own history with its own pioneers and celebrities. You should find out about them and be interested in their views. Also, who are your rivals and peers within the sector and how do they operate? What are *their* histories? Which organization is *the* organization for the sector? How did they get there? Meanwhile, who's in crisis? And where does your organization stand in such a league table?

All sectors will have specialist magazines that can help us, although we should use such publications like text books – taking notes and revising the information – rather than as something to browse and forget.

And if you read the above and think: "you know what, I just can't be bothered to find out about the history of the Birmingham widget industry and its rivals in Germany and China. I'd rather read my motorcycle maintenance magazine" then you might just have answered the question about whether you are at the foot of the right ladder, as well as what ladder might be the one to seek out.

When opportunity knocks, open the door

All this research should give you strong ammunition to strike when opportunity knocks, usually in the form of the office crisis. As Goldsmith says, the office problem – as well as its big brother the office crisis – are major opportunity moments for any worker. Suddenly we are in the right place at the right time – on hand with the hose to douse the flames. Yet we must know that it's the hose we need, and be able to handle it. Otherwise we are a long way from being in the right place at the right time. We are simply in the way.

Having said this, not all of the problems are of the *"fire, fire!"* sort. Many are positive moments of opportunity for the organization: how best to market a new product, or take advantage of a crisis at a rival firm, or deal with your line manager's new post-promotion responsibilities.

Become the boss's adviser

In *Why Should the Boss Listen to You?* (2008) strategic adviser James Lukaszewski sets out the traits required to get ourselves on the fastest known conveyor to goal achievement within any organization – to be the CEO's (or anyone senior's) trusted adviser.

"What matters to leaders is success," writes Lukaszewski. "They will pay attention to you if they think you have a good sense of what they need to achieve that success."

To succeed as an advisor to the senior executives, says Lukaszewski, you must get involved in projects that appeal to them – providing solid ideas as well as small suggestions. You must not be selfish. Your aim should be to aid their needs rather than nakedly advance your own. Yet you must be curious – identifying, investigating and mastering new and perhaps misunderstood information. And you must keep your ego in check.

Key steps to winning the boss's ear, according to Lukaszewski, include:

- *Being trustworthy* – unless executives know you are onside, can keep secrets and have sound judgement, they are unlikely to turn to you for help.
- *Becoming a verbal visionary* – words are a CEO's "stock in trade" so use language that creates visions and inspires (and be proud when they adopt it as their own).
- *Developing a management perspective* – situations look very different to a boss looking down upon the shopfloor. You need to show the CEO you understand this and can adapt your viewpoint.
- *Being a window to tomorrow* – focus on the future of the company, what you can do today to build tomorrow.
- *Advising constructively* – the phrase "constructive criticism" is an oxymoron for Lukaszewski as negative comments will stop the person listening (and the CEO may turn elsewhere for advice). You need to recast criticism in positive, helpful terms so you are heard (this may take practice). Certainly, when a senior seeks your opinion, it is most usually no more than an invitation to agree, no matter how it is worded.

High-FFs and delegation

Delegation is another key requirement for progress, and is another one of those traumatic areas for those with a high fear of failure, especially when in a junior role. Many junior High-FFs fear delegation because they are suspicious of the motives involved – both of your boss who has instructed you to delegate, perhaps to undermine you, and of your colleague, who may seem overly keen to learn your job and take over. We may also fail to see training others as your role. We have a full workload and are unlikely to be assessed on how well we "make ourselves redundant" (to use the unhelpful phrase adopted by one of my seniors).

So what are we to do? Our best, that's what.

It's massively self-defeating to assume the worst. If it's true, it'll happen anyway. Perhaps being outmanoeuvred and "let go" is just what we need at this stage. We have our long-term goals in place and we were clearly on the wrong path or, at the very least, working for the wrong boss or organization. Yet by assuming it is true and behaving accordingly it is, yet again, self-fulfilling.

And by effectively delegating to others you are showing confidence in yourself, as well as freeing up your time for more important work, although you mustn't make the common mistake of retaining the grunt work while delegating the more creative and exciting stuff because the results are less certain or "it'll save time." Being able to delegate means you've done your time on the grunt work and you're on your way up, so if you hand over the creative stuff you've just anchored yourself to the floor while sending your colleague up the ladder.

Commit to the organization

One thing we must do is commit to the organization we work for or find one we can commit to and do whatever it takes to get in the door. This could include initially doing the wrong job for the right organization. In the bank, for instance, I noticed that many of the female executives had started as PAs and many men and women had joined at 16 as lowly branch cashiers. And my first post-university job was selling classified ads for *The Independent*, simply because I wanted to work on a national newspaper.

I hated the work less than I thought – in fact was surprisingly good at it (and have used the sales training ever since) – and meanwhile looked for editorial opportunities, despite being told such a move was impossible. These came in the form of articles on the environment for the youth section and, soon enough, a full-time opening came, although with a much reduced salary and the requirement to learn some editorial production skills (which I have also used ever since). Whatever the compromises, it was a great thrill to win my first ever payslip as a journalist, finally feeling that I was at the foot of the right ladder.

Yet I still gave everything to the classified ads job in an attempt to enhance my reputation within the organization – knowing that being judged well was crucial, no matter what the task. According to management academic Charles E. Watson in *What Smart People do When Dumb Things Happen at Work* (1999) superior performers put service to others before self-interest, especially as – according to Watson – every organization is constantly involved in a weeding out process, continually separating those who produce meaningful results from those who simply go through the motions.

To avoid such a fate you should, according to Watson:

- Seek and understand the big picture behind your projects and be motivated by that big picture.
- Focus on the work, not the rewards it may bring (this includes money).
- Live by your word – promoting trust in you.
- Keep your commitments and meet your deadlines, even if you incur costs (in time or money).

Of course, throughout this you should stay laser-focused on the short – and medium-term goals that help you meet your long-term objectives. Judge every task, every meeting, every project, every evaluation, every interaction – and definitely every day – on the basis of whether you are moving towards your objectives. Yet be flexible. You have 10 years to meet your ultimate goals so a compromise today may position you well for tomorrow, while intransigence may set you back years.

"Thank God it's today"

Richard Carlson is also very relevant in coping with the work environment – so relevant he wrote a specific book on it entitled *Don't Sweat the Small Stuff at Work* (1998). Key homilies include "never, ever backstab," "remember to appreciate the people you work with," "ease off your ego," "don't sweat the demanding boss," "learn to say no without guilt," "strengthen your presence," "make friends with the receptionists" and "don't let negative coworkers get you down" – all of which make total sense without much need for additional thought.

One – called "join my new club: *TGIT*" – perhaps requires further explanation. This is an attack on two sorts of worker – the *Thank God it's Friday* gang that live for the weekend, hate Mondays and are likely to have empty work lives; and the *Thank God it's Monday* gang that have no life but their work, hate the weekends and consider the "demands" of their family or friends an intrusion.

"Needless to say," says Carlson. "Members of both clubs think the members of the other club are completely nuts!"

He invites us to join the *Thank God it's Today* club in which we bask in the uniqueness and beauty of each day of the week.

"As simple as it seems, the desire to maintain a membership in this club can make a substantial difference in the attitude you carry with you to work and in fact all life," says Carlson.

A final Carlson recommendation worth noting is to "make the best of your non-creative position," which suggests you have a choice regarding any job you may consider something of a drudge. You can dread the tasks, or you can decide to enjoy them and make best use of them.

He used two bricklayers as an example – one resentfully piling bricks on top of each other "in the hot sun" while the other marvelling at the "beautiful structures" he was creating, although it reminded me of the Detroit car workers who used the mind-numbing hours on the production line to invent and test the tunes and lyrics that became the *Motown* sound – proving that even the most *soul*-destroying work is anything but if we adopt the right attitude.

Case Study 14 – The poor delegator

Joseph worked in design. He thought he was very good at it, as did his employers. He informed me of this in a long email after reading the first edition of *What's Stopping You?* In fact, he was seen as so good, he wrote, that he needed virtually no supervision from the agency owners after just a few months at the company. And before long he was running important accounts on his own.

So why was he writing to me? Because he couldn't delegate, and he was concerned it had cost him his career.

The company had taken on a junior and asked Joseph to mentor him. At first, he saw this as a compliment – that he'd been trusted to nurture new talent. Yet he had no patience to help the new designer, so found himself saying: "don't worry, I'll do it," whenever there was a difficulty or something needed presenting to the client in a particular way.

Instead, he gave the designer the "blue sky" projects that required his full creativity – leaving Joseph with the routine work simply because he knew how to do it and thought it was more efficient to "get it done."

Of course, Joseph could see his mistake – rooting himself to the floor while allowing the junior to rise through the ranks on "get noticed" projects. And he wondered if his troubled South London upbringing – with a single mother battling poverty and an abusive and estranged biological father who had another family in a different part of London – had made him distrustful of others: hence the enquiry to me.

Indeed, the new designer soon won public praise, which made Joseph irrationally angry. Yet rather than battle his own negative and self-sabotaging responses to the need for nurturing a team, he sought a way out. He resigned in order to go freelance.

Joseph being Joseph brooded on this decision – for a while seeing it as self-sabotage: a cop out, perhaps, or running away from responsibility. Yet the work flowed in and, after a time, he realized that nurturing others was just not his thing.

"Freelancing is great because I can focus on the bits of the work I like and leave the bits I like less to others," he said.

Joseph was also keen to pursue other interests, potentially going back to college. That said, he seemed well aware of the damage poor delegation had inflicted on his more formal career pursuits, although was managing to rationalize his thoughts and actions.

"I had to make a decision regarding what I was prepared to do and what I wasn't," he said.

What's Stopping You? *Commit to the organization you work for or find one you can commit to and do what it takes to get in the door – even initially doing the wrong job. You must understand your organization and learn to delegate. But you must always stay focused on your long-term objectives.*

15

NETWORKING
AND INTERVIEWS

No matter how hard you try, at some point you may have to accept that you are in the wrong organization. At the foot of the wrong ladder. What then? As stated, doing the wrong job in the right building is a good start – but how do we get even that far?

A crucial requirement for anyone seeking to make progress both within and beyond their own organization will be to develop a good network of contacts. Networking is one of those aspects of work life that tend to make non-ambitious or anti-business people cringe. Yet far from hating networking, many disparagers actually fear it.

This is probably based on their success or otherwise when dealing with their peers in the playground – the place where the concept of networks and hierarchies among peers first arises. Certainly, I had playground exclusion issues: I just wasn't big or tough enough to make the top gang. These feelings were compounded at university, where I wasn't cool enough, and compounded as a young graduate in the media industry, where I didn't seem to be posh enough. But while all these groups and hierarchies are true, they are nearly all based on childish or youthful notions of elitism that are unsophisticated at best and, in the workplace, completely inappropriate if not rather pathetic.

Forget playground experiences

As grown-ups we should simply forget all those past experiences. Networking in the work environment may look and feel like the playground but it's actually the opposite. We are dealing with an entirely different group of people incentivized in an entirely different way. Plug into what makes people tick in this setting, and we should be away.

While being tough in the playground or cool at university is a vital element for success in those environments, because they are based on exclusivity, in the workplace – meanwhile – being plugged into the machine is the key need. Everybody needs to know everybody, and those ambitious High-AMs are equally aware of this. Therefore, the very people that may have intimidated us at school and university for their skills at topping hierarchies, are now the ones that need to learn a new skill: collaboration.

Being aloof in an organization – at least when you're a junior – makes no sense at all. And very few High-FFs are aloof or arrogant (although plenty are shy, which can be mistaken as such). This means we already have half the skills we need when in any networking situation, we are approachable – at least when we're not frowning with anger or fear. The other need, of course, is for the confidence to approach others. And it is here where we need help.

Generating rapport

In *Network Your Way to Success* (2002), marketing director John Timperley offers a development plan for connecting us with our peers and, most importantly, creating rapport from those connections.

"Put simply," says Timperley, "if you have the ability to generate rapport with others, you'll be happy and successful; if you don't, you won't. Without rapport in your networking you'll just be going through the motions."

Rapport building sounds like the sort of skill lacked by those with fear of failure while innately found within those with high achievement motivation – meaning that High-FFs shy away from most networking opportunities or just stand back and watch while the High-AMs rapport away. But there's no need. This is not the playground. The very fact we are in the building or at this particular event means, in some way or other, we are a cog in the machine. And most people worth talking to want to know how the machine works and who the cogs are – giving you the chance to introduce yourself by explaining who you are and what role you play.

Of course, some may not be interested in how the machine works and blank or even belittle you. But that's just them declaring themselves out of the game. Most are embittered High-FFs not wanting to change: seeing everyone else as a threat and hating the very machine that feeds them, or being over-protective of their own tiny enclave. You just need to move on and thank heavens you have avoided such a fate or stay and try and engage anyway – avoiding becoming the preaching motivational convert, of course.

Networking potential

Networking opportunities are many and varied and we should be constantly alive to their potential in any situation. In an office this includes our immediate desk environment, as well as on the introductory tour around our department. It can also include real or manufactured reasons for visiting other departments, loo and water-cooler breaks (and door huddles if we smoke), meeting room events, or requirements to visit the management suite. All can deliver results – remembering Carlson's plea to "make friends with receptionists" as well as other support staff. A surprising number of support staff have the ear of seniors and most are gatekeepers of one sort or another.

And for both employees, as well as those freelancing or working alone, researching and attending networking events is an important requirement. At work, lobbying to attend such events shows commitment, enthusiasm and a willingness to learn. Indeed, for everyone, such events link us into our sector more effectively than just about any other route.

Timperley has some strong tips for developing good rapport with others at such an event, and elsewhere. You should (with added thoughts of my own):

- *Smile* – however forced, it is better than a frown in making you approachable. You should practise your smile in front of the mirror, making sure it lights up your face to the point where it looks like you mean it.

- *Put them in the spotlight* – be interested in who you meet. Who cares whether you have got your vital points across? In fact, by listening you have – you have informed them you are interested in them, which is crucial for good networking. In *What They Don't Teach You at Harvard Business School,* Mark McCormack writes that the ability to listen, and to "really hear what someone is saying" has greater business implications than simply "gaining insight" into people. He cites Pepsi wrestling the Burger King account from Coke only once they started properly listening to the client.

- *Mirroring* – broadly mirror the person's body language, although not to the point of freaking them out. You don't need the NLPer's intensity in this but, by adopting the same general posture, speed of speech, arm placement – that sort of thing – you can build unconscious rapport. Certainly, body language is vital when you first meet new people. According to Mark McCormack people are constantly revealing themselves through conscious (e.g. dress) or unconscious (e.g. body language) signals. But this is a two-way street, meaning you should both observe and signal.

- *Dress to impress* – forget attempts at individualism and adopt "group norms" says Timperley. And in the world of work this means dress. While different sectors have different uniforms, most office work involves the standard office attire (either suits or smart casual). And for men that also means being clean-shaven, avoiding wacky piercings, tattoos, jewellery or hair products. Female uniforms are more subtle but are still worth noting and observing. The way female executives dress, for instance, is usually very different to that of PAs and receptionists. And the clothes you wear to work should look like they are meant for work – not for impressing potential conquests in a nightclub. Of course, creative industries have trendier uniforms – perhaps including piercings, tattoos and facial hair. But, even here, understating your appearance – at least until you are established – is better than an outrageous affectation that, if you shoot wide, could undermine rather than build your confidence.

- *Seek to understand and seek to empathize* – no matter what they are saying and how far it may diverge from your own perspective, you are not there to argue but to win people over. As Richard Carlson says, no matter what their view, you should agree with them – "just for fun."

- *Use names* – Timperley cites Dale Carnegie's line that a person's name is the "sweetest sound anyone ever hears," so you should make efforts to remember people's names. One trick I was taught in sales training was to repeat back someone's name immediately you are introduced. "Hi I'm Daphne," she says. "Hello Daphne, how are you?" we say back. Of course, you may have to say Daphne a few times for it to lodge and you shouldn't use it so often it unnerves them.

- *Make contacts feel special* – this works across the board when dealing with people. As High-FFs we are so inwardly focused – so often wrapped up in our own feelings of insecurity – that we forget that the most effective thing we can do in any people situation is to make the other person feel like the valued one. Pay subtle compliments – it's the best sales tool known to man.

- *Introduce yourself well* – practise a good intro. For instance, if you say something like: "Hi – I'm the boring one you won't want to talk to" you'll quickly prove yourself right. Don't lie, of course, but focus on the positive, or make a joke. "Hi – I've just started in waste management – boy is that sector in need of a clean up!" OK, maybe not that one.

- *Be warm* – Tipperley states that your opening line can be virtually anything as long as it is delivered warmly and puts people at their ease.

- *Shake hands* – in most situations it is polite to offer a handshake, but take note of the norms in the room. Avoid the *"mwah, mwah"* kissing unless it is *de rigueur* in your industry, and even then don't over assume – it is often intended as a greeting for insiders. And those handshakes – every book I read insists on a firm handshake, so I will do the opposite and warn against the bone-crusher. A gentle squeeze is fine – too firm and you can come across as a rookie salesman.

- *Use space effectively* – this is a difficult one for me as I suffer a bit from cocktail party syndrome, which means that noisy situations make hearing difficult. I try to stand back but lean in, which – of course – has the added benefit of projecting attentiveness. Otherwise, Tipperley offers the insight that standing next to someone facing the same way but with aligned body-language can be both informal and "sharing" and is better than the more adversarial face-to-face.

- *Reveal yourself* – all that listening means you should offer something of yourself, or they may feel interrogated. Be open, you have nothing to hide. I have also found the line "I'm new and keen to build up my network of contacts in the industry" a disarming gambit that often has people keen to prove they are a worthy contact.

Networking don'ts

And there are some clear "don'ts" when it comes to both networking and office behaviour generally, of which number one is "don't mix sex and networking." Being overly flirty changes the dynamic of a conversation, alienates everyone else in the group, is unprofessional and destroys reputations faster than any other trait bar theft or violence. Even if it appears to be initially successful, by using the prospect of sex as a means of advancement you are announcing that you have no other skills worth considering and should be judged as such.

Success by this route means being disliked and disrespected by your colleagues at all levels, which will ultimately place limits on your prospects. Let the cocky High-AMs trip up on this one. We High-FFs should watch, learn and avoid.

For other "don'ts" we should turn to Dale Carnegie's famous tome *How to Win Friends and Influence People*, originally published in the 1930s.

"Criticisms are like homing pigeons, they always return home," writes Carnegie.

Being nice about people was his first and most important principle. And it is especially true when networking. I have made some terrible gaffes from trying to be interesting and funny, and sound like an insider, by repeating some gossip or criticism I heard about an industry name – or even just repeating an unflattering nickname – only for it to get back to them and for two contacts and my reputation to be damaged.

Bitching is a High-FF trait based on our own insecurities. It is also one we should actively suppress.

"Any fool can criticize, condemn and complain," says Carnegie, "and most fools do. But it takes character and self-control to be understanding and forgiving."

Carnegie also implores us to avoid arguments, show respect, see the other's point of view, begin in a friendly way (even if angry) and to try and get a "yes" at the beginning of a conversation – any yes.

Yet all this networking needs to have some impact, doesn't it? Well no. As long as we are on the right ladder knowing other industry insiders is a dividend in itself. Contacts are like ripples in a lake, each fanning out to hit every shore at some point. Sales, jobs, partnerships, staff, publicity – all may come to you from some distant shore at some distant date, thanks to the ripples started from one conversation.

Should any openings come up . . .

But contacts are pebbles thrown in the lake, not rocks. You should therefore temper your expectations. If you want them to offer you a job you may need to throw rocks – i.e. directly state your intentions to those you want to work for (although never do this at a networking event).

Your rocks, however, should be well targeted. You should actively research the organization you want to work for, source the right person and focus your attention on that person, although, again, you should temper your expectations – just offering a polite note that, while your current employment is fruitful, your ultimate aim is to join the leading/most innovative/largest or whatever organization in the sector and, should any openings come up in the foreseeable future . . .

Avoid desperation, over-baking the cake, pompous jargon or sycophancy. This is simply one professional communicating to another about their preferred intentions. And avoid being seen as a runaway. As an employer I now ask every person I interview whether they are simply running away from their current job. Like philanderers, and some murderers, runaways tend to encourage the prefix "serial."

Dealing with interviews

Yet again this process involves another major hurdle for those with a high fear of failure: interviews. And interviews. To become a banker I had to endure three informal meetings, four formal interviews, a dinner, two lunches, two major drinking sessions and a weekend offsite in the Home Counties (and that's not counting the speech at the annual offsite, delivered in both New York and London). And despite my High-FF propensity for exaggeration I'm afraid this is not only true, it is no more than the norm for most key senior appointments in an age where recruitment mistakes can be crippling.

In *Great Answers to Tough Interview Questions* (2001), Martin John Yate (author of the *Knock 'em Dead . . .* series of books) states that your aim in interviews should be to offer concrete proof of your suitability based on experience and skills. Even college volunteering or internships can be presented to support the requirements of the post although "an untruth or exaggeration could cost you a job." Certainly, references to thin experience are better than saying you are enthusiastic or a quick learner, both of which are meaningless.

Avoiding self-sabotage

Unfortunately, job interviews are the very occasions High-FFs can reveal one of their most harmful traits – self-sabotage. Nervous and fearful, we can find ourselves not only revealing our weaknesses but readily volunteering them – even going out of our way to state them. Certainly, this is an area that has generated some of my most cringe-worthy moments, as well as some of the monkey's greatest victories.

* *Volunteering weakness.* One interview with the well-known editor of a national newspaper involves me telling him I knew nothing about finance and wouldn't want to work on that section! This was the very area I was later to focus on, but not for this editor – who thought me an idiot for volunteering my weaknesses. He left me to his deputy, who showed me the door soon after.

- *Disagreeing.* Another opening on a national newspaper. So proudly had I adopted my university city of Manchester that I'd ventured a criticism that the paper had ignored a large but ultimately pointless protest march about some long-forgotten cause. He responded defensively but, rather than spot this and retreat, I kept going until he firmly stated "I'm sure we considered it" – his irritation now obvious.

Yet self-sabotage can begin even before the actual interview.

- *The undermining CV.* One interviewer pointed out that I'd listed "politics" under my interests. "As long as you don't bring it to work," he said. Yet I was doing a degree in politics (this was for a holiday job), so why did I feel the need to state this potentially undermining "interest" on my CV? He worried I'd bore him senseless with extremist diatribes, and he was probably right. But why couldn't he have found this out three months in and with my more positive attributes outweighing my negatives?
- *Acting the slob.* Early for one pre-university interview, I thought I had time for a cigarette outside. With no matches I asked the professional-looking gentleman walking by. Even in the 1980s he looked an unlikely smoker, and seemed taken aback by the request. Yet he did look like my likely interviewer, which – of course – he was. He was distinctly unimpressed, and I learnt a painful lesson regarding reigning in the oikish behaviour long before the interviewer's door.

Indeed, interviews can be major barriers for High-FFs, although once we know the rules of the game such barriers are easily surmountable. For instance, Yate warns that many interview questions are a trap, including (again with added interpretation):

- *What are your least favourite office chores?* The interviewer is trying to calculate your maturity – rebuff it with positive statements about acquiring valuable skills "even from routine tasks."

- *How did you choose your university?* The interviewer is trying to establish whether you are a stay-at-homer or have some drive.
- *How was your tuition funded?* Mention any part time jobs to avoid looking like a "trustafarian" (a UK term for someone with a private income).
- *What were the highs and lows of the last job?* The interviewer is trying to spot the runaways. Be positive about the last job but say this opportunity fits even better and is the next step.
- *Why are you earning so little?* This is perhaps the only enquiry that can be politely thrown back. At my age, experience is more important than money, you can say, but what should I be earning (although money and benefits chats should wait for the offer)?

In the interview, Yate warns against "constant head bobbing syndrome" – offering the head tilt and occasional slow nod as an alternative, and he is not keen on grinning or hand usage that may give covert signals. These include pen tapping (impatience), hands clasped behind head (smugness), collar tugging (lying) and hands in pockets with thumbs out (aggression). Eye contact is good but don't stare. Mirroring is good but don't freak them out. Taking notes is good (and helps prevent overdoing both the eye contact and mirroring) but don't write verbatim.

In sales training I was taught that the aim of the call was not to get a sale. It was to get the next call. The aim of the second call? To get a meeting. The aim of the meeting? To get a second meeting. The aim of the second meeting? To get the sale by the third meeting. Remember that you are simply trying to get to the next stage – don't rush the process but be grateful if you avoid three informal meetings, four formal interviews, a dinner . . .

Case Study 15 – Bamboozled by one-to-ones

"It's the one-to-ones that get me," said Frank.

He'd attended one of my fear of failure evenings and approached me at the end. Now 50 (my guess), he said he'd had a good career – working in the compliance department of a major financial institution. He was well plugged into his sector, he said – going to conferences on regulation and money laundering and even occasionally chairing a panel discussion.

"I have no problem in front of an audience," he said. "I can focus on what I'm saying – especially when talking about what I know."

"But put me in front of one person and I become flustered and paranoid and that can even lead to anger," he said.

Most frustratingly for Frank, this had destroyed his ability to progress in his career due to what he saw as poor behaviour when being interviewed.

"I just assume they think I'm an idiot," he said. "I get defensive – annoyed even. I can't bear the idea of being judged. It makes me clam up or – worse – say something stupid."

Frank felt this one problem – his inability to get over feelings of defensiveness when facing another person – had dogged his entire life. He felt like a small animal, he said, fearing attack the entire time.

And this went way beyond job interviews. He assumed shop assistants, mechanics and other tradespeople thought him a fool. He'd look for signs they were mocking him and become convinced they had nothing but contempt for his needs – perhaps not thinking his custom important. He expected to be ripped off or even openly belittled, with even greengrocers and newsagents generating neural hijackings by asking the most perfunctory of questions.

I asked if he'd ever considered counselling. He'd been, he said, but it had been poor quality in his view.

"He was obsessed by the fact my father was violently abusive when I was a child," he said, raising his eyebrows.

"Do *you* think there's a connection?" I asked.

"Probably," he said after a pause and with a wistful smile that failed to hide the emotion now welling up inside him.

"It's the one-to-ones that get me," he repeated after another brief silence, before excusing himself for the bathroom.

I was talking to someone else when he came out, but I caught him just before he left.

"I'm no psychotherapist," I said, "but my guess is you need to find a therapist you trust and respect – perhaps female – and try again."

What's Stopping You? *Strong networking is essential in any career and is achievable once you understand the dynamics. You are not there to prove yourself but to win people over – so don't expect any immediate dividend. In interviews, even thin experiences are better than meaningless promises.*

16

LEADERSHIP

Leadership is a strange concept for those with high fear of failure. To progress we will almost certainly have to manage people, build teams, give instruction: *lead*. Leadership may be thrust upon us – and must be if we are to progress. Yet, as High-FFs, we have none of the natural faculties of leadership and will, in fact, have a lot of the faculties that suggests we should avoid taking charge of others. Leadership, for those with a high fear of failure, can seem like a contradiction in terms.

Yet, like goal achievement, leadership is possible as long as we are prepared to accept who we are – including our faulty wiring – and externalize and depersonalize our experiences. If we can remove our obsession with our immediate selves – by thinking, instead, of the longer-term *Me Inc.* – we can become highly effective leaders.

Simply defined, leadership is goal achievement for a group of individuals with you at the helm. All teams have objectives and, as its leader, you need to be fully onboard with those goals. And if they are *your* goals, then leadership is no more than the recruitment of others in pursuit of them, which is a fantastic turnaround for High-FFs more used to being recruited by those with high achievement motivation to help pursue *their* goals.

Given that you are the guardian and guarantor of your own achievements, therefore, you should, first, acquire some leadership skills and, second, lose your fear of exercising them. In fact "exercising" is a good word because we get better at management with practice. I have been managing people in one form or another for 17 years and cringe at some of my earlier fumblings. They were – based on my insecurities and paranoia – tactless, clumsy, selfish, and appallingly instructed and executed. *Sorry!*

Leadership suits the High-FF

Luckily for those around me I am marginally better today, not least because the world is moving the way of the High-FF when it comes to leadership. According to corporate transformation expert Manfred Kets de Vries in *The Leadership Mystique* (2001) business leaders have traditionally been trained to focus on "hard data and cold logic" – considering "soft" matters such as emotion and intuition as immeasurable in terms of output so, in management terms, irrelevant. And, indeed, emotional issues tend to be underlying and difficult to see, and therefore especially difficult to manage.

Yet ignoring soft matters can harm your prospects as a leader, says Kets de Vries.

"Emotional intelligence plays a vital role in the leadership equation," he says. "It comes down to this: people who are emotionally intelligent are more likely to be effective as leaders."

This takes us right back to Daniel Goleman's book *Emotional Intelligence* and his focus on EQ. Yet, by the time we have moved up the ladder to the point of leading a team, things have moved in the High-FF's favour, especially in the modern world. Most people reading this book will work in the knowledge economy. This is the world of the office or studio and it involves people who possess both skills and choices. We are a long way from the industrialized workforce of the last century – with workers undertaking fractional and brainless tasks and productivity measured purely in quantitative output.

Productivity in the modern economy involves qualitative measurements such as creativity, thought leadership, analysis and mental processing. And this requires humans who are emotionally – as well as intellectually – capable of performing such tasks. It also requires leaders who can motivate workers through emotional awareness and intelligence.

A new approach to leadership

As de Vries puts it, the old leadership model of "command, control and compliance" has been replaced by the new model of "ideas, information and interaction." The old paternal model of lifetime employment and lifetime loyalty has been replaced by a more adult relationship, which is a major revolution in management needs and one that – surprisingly – plays right into our hands as recovering High-FFs.

But we must learn how to capitalize upon it. Our self-obsession may prevent us from seeing that, as High-FFs, our previous weaknesses – of being too emotional, too sensitive, of being overly concerned with not losing face, of giving too much credence to external opinions – becomes our strengths. Yet, to lead, we must externalize these experiences and see it from the viewpoint of others, especially those we lead.

Certainly, High-FF leadership seems counterintuitive until we step through the mirror. Once through, our experiences – if we can learn from them – give us a strong understanding of the needs of the people we lead. The experiences of those with high achievement motivation, however, render them clueless.

The crucial ability: empathy

In *Working with Emotional Intelligence*, the 1998 follow-up to *Emotional Intelligence*, Daniel Goleman states that our ability to empathize with the emotional needs of others is crucial in the modern world of work – an essential building block in business leadership that underlies our ability to be a mentor and to navigate sometimes conflicting workplace personalities.

Optimal productivity requires strong interpersonal relationships, he says, that we may ruin if we fail to pay enough attention to the emotional impact of our decisions on those we lead. And while this can trip up ambitious High-AMs, who are solely focused on achievement motivation, the insecurities we carry as recovering High-FFs should give us an awareness of the hierarchy below – as well as a sensitivity – that should work in our favour, as long as we are intelligent enough to realize that the emotions we felt on the way up are the same now being felt by our team.

Goleman's key point is that the people we lead are at least as important as the people we follow, despite their lower position in the hierarchy. And this means that – just for once – our insecurities as High-FFs, where we are so often concerned about what people think of us or how we are being perceived, is on-the-money when it comes to leadership. Yet, extraordinarily, this is the very moment, with the very people, that High-FFs can decide to become insensitive. Once in the boss's camp of achievement motivation, many High-FFs feel they should adopt High-AM ways – perhaps by focusing solely on goal achievement rather than on listening to their team – which is a disaster because, in this instance, the High-AM should be adopting the thinking of the High-FF.

The paradox of success

Marshall Goldsmith (with Mark Reiter) addresses this very concern in his book *What Got You Here Won't Get You There* (2008). In what he calls the "paradox of success," Goldsmith explains that the same beliefs and behaviours that made people successful can create problems when they lead.

Ironically, problem behaviours can include "winning too much," which makes them trample over others, "adding too much value," which prevents others getting any credit, "passing judgement," which means offering opinions rather than listening, "being straight talking" which means making destructive comments and being too critical, and "telling the world how smart they are," rather than offering praise to others.

These are all traits that those with high achievement motivation have used to get to the top. Now there, however, they can alienate the team below them and destroy confidence, creativity, optimism and, ultimately, loyalty. Little wonder that so many High-AMs, when made the boss, simply keep going: acquiring companies, becoming corporate raiders, throwing themselves into maniacal deal-doing and even becoming crooks. Anything but nurture the team beneath them.

In fact, we only need to understand the word "leadership" to see the error. It isn't advanced "followship" up the hierarchy or across to larger peers. It's our ability to inspire the people in the hierarchy below that matters.

One minute management

So how best to achieve this? In my view the single most effective action we can take as a strong leader is to back off. In the *One Minute Manager* (1983) management trainer Ken Blanchard (with Spencer Johnson) sets out to prove that less is more when it comes to team instruction. What happens in those all-important 60 seconds is not instruction or management by the leader, but the setting out of an agreed vision regarding the result of a project or task. How they arrive at this result is up to those charged with execution. This leaves the team incentivized to complete the task as best they can. It is *their* task after all, and they should get *all* the credit.

Blanchard's style of management is aimed at building confidence and a sense of ownership. With such autonomy the leader hasn't simply let go – Blanchard builds in additional elements such as the *One Minute Reprimands* or *One Minute Praisings* if the manager needs to intervene (although the reprimands, at least, should be executed sparingly). Yet by showing such a sense of trust in their team, the leader has unleashed the team's full potential to reward that empowerment.

Make others feel important

But there are also more engaged leadership traits. In *How to Win Friends and Influence People*, Dale Carnegie states that one of the most important traits in any influential person is making other people feel important. No matter how young or inexperienced our team, this is a strong basic desire among all human beings and, as a team leader, we have the power to inject others with that feeling.

Another Carnegie recommendation is to offer praise liberally. This doesn't have to be when undeserved, although even when reprimanding the management concept of the "sh*t sandwich" is a good one (the idea of first stating what's good, then tackling the problems, before ending on a positive note). Yet praise should be fulsome and meant, not delivered through gritted teeth.

In my opinion praise is the second most valuable currency after money – in fact, used wisely, it can go where money can't. For all but the most greedy, money is an avoidance commodity. Most people, especially when young, are avoiding not earning money rather than actively working to accumulate wealth. As stated, what most people seek is a sense of achievement or well-being – of being valued as important. And in this respect the currency they value is praise. As a leader you should value the criticism you receive (a difficult task for the High-FF, admittedly) but you should also value the praise that you give: it is far more important than the criticism.

Maslow's hierarchy of needs

If this seems far-fetched then we simply need to refer to Maslow's hierarchy of needs. Abraham Maslow was interested in exemplary people and their motivations, which turned into a theory of human needs and self-actualization. Usually expressed as a pyramid, Maslow in his 1943 paper *A Theory of Human Motivation* states that humans move up from the basic physiological needs for food and water to require safety in the form of shelter, employment and health. Above that humans need friendship and love, and above that self-esteem, confidence, achievement and respect. And at the very top of the pyramid are attributes such as morality and creativity. At all levels money is simply a means to an end.

This is an enlightening concept for any team leader, and far more powerful than a pay scale – not least because it is apparent that humans cannot graduate to the next level without satisfying the needs of the lower level. Only once we have food and water can we

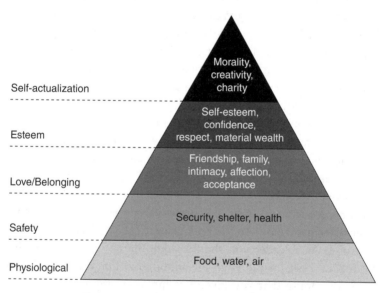

Figure 16.1 Maslow's hierarchy of needs

think about shelter and security. Only once we have safety can we think about love and belonging. Only once we are loved can we think about self-esteem and respect. And only once we have self-respect do we crave morality.

Apply this to both yourself and your team, and it is apparent that those in most modern offices have moved beyond the safety level. Most, hopefully, will also have well-developed feelings of love and belonging – although this may well be the level where many High-FFs, due to childhood experiences, have become trapped – preventing them moving up to the level of self-esteem and confidence. You cannot offer the love they seek in this respect but you can offer the belonging, which should improve their confidence and desire for achievement, making your team highly motivated. And this, in turn, will reinforce your own sense of belonging as a recovering High-FF.

Generating a sense of security for a team, via autonomy and praise, is therefore far more powerful than operating on a system of fear and rewards: the sack or riches. It is also a lot easier to deliver.

The hiring gambit

But what if you regard your team with such contempt you cannot offer such autonomy? What if they are not worthy of your praise? Well you may have the wrong team. In fact, this is a likely scenario. High-FFs are notorious for hiring the wrong people. We look for individuals that will not challenge our seemingly tenuous grip on authority – instead hiring people we feel have "the right attitude." We may occasionally fool ourselves into thinking we can handle star players but we will soon convince ourselves – through crises, real or imagined – that we have no room for "prima donnas," especially not ones that seem to threaten our position.

Certainly, one-minute management is impossible without a degree of confidence in our team, so our first task may need to be some strong hiring. Yet employing someone – especially for the first time – is a key moment for the recovering High-FF: we have to have the courage of our convictions here and build a team that will help us achieve our goals.

In his seminar-turned-book *Crazy Times Call for Crazy Organizations*, Tom Peters writes with regards to company recruitment (and much else besides):

"Most organizations bore me stiff."

Peters is trying to create the "curious corporation," as – in his way – is Blanchard. Can you create and lead the curious team? The answer is that you must, if you are to create an effective team to pursue your goals. Otherwise you will keep hiring personal assistants that, when they discover their station, will resent you and, at best, quit – leaving you back at square one. At worst they will make your most paranoid fantasies self-fulfilling.

Spotting curious people

If we therefore agree with Tom Peters that curious people are the way ahead, how do we spot them and persuade them to join? In fact, this is the easy bit.

"I think that Rule No.1 in the corporate recruiting manual is, 'Thou shalt not hire anyone who has as much as a nanosecond's gap in her or his resume [CV] between nursery school and now,'" says Peters.

Most hirers look for people with the perfect CV – good grades, a good university, strong experience in the right places and no awkward bits that might need an explanation. It is the IBM factor for people ("nobody ever got fired for hiring IBM," is a famous business quote). Yet Peters is saying we may be looking down the wrong end of the telescope. People who have travelled or who have otherwise wayward CVs may be the very people we need. They may even be fellow High-FFs who are also, like us, rattling the cage in frustration. If we can determine that this is not just another job, that they see this as the foot of the right ladder, then, as long as we can inspire and motivate them, we are likely to uncover some gems.

"Hire a few genuine off-the-wall sorts," he says, "collect some weirdos."

What Peters is really saying is that being a paranoid hirer may look safe, but can be costly. And that the odd leap of faith in unconventional people could well be highly rewarding – not least because of the loyalty we can build by taking young, talented but directionless people and giving them a sense of direction: especially a direction – thanks to Blanchard – that they largely forge for themselves. Certainly, this has been my experience at *Moorgate*.

It won't always work

Yet for every hire that works, there is another that doesn't. In this respect, the recruiter needs to go easy on themselves. People are people and not everyone is going to buy into your vision, no matter what they say at the interview or how strongly we try and incentivize them.

We have our objectives and we should focus on those and those alone. If someone is just not on the same page – after strong and repeated attempts by you to motivate them – then you should both move on, seeing each recruiting failure as a step towards recruiting success.

Having said this, it is right that you see each recruiting failure as *your* failure and something *you* have to learn from. Hiring is a skill you have to hone. One common mistake I made in my early days was to hire based on avoiding my last hiring mistake – looking for the person that the previous guy wasn't, which was another way of not taking responsibility for my recruiting failures. Another common mistake was to always look for the cultural fit. Yet, while hiring clones is a quick way to confirm our own prejudices, we need individuals from a range of backgrounds who won't necessarily agree with us or each other. If we are sensitive High-FFs unable to cope with criticism then we will decapitate our team's potential.

Inspiring leadership

Listening to your team and acting accordingly inspires loyalty. In fact, "inspire" is an important word because that's what good leaders do – it is their key attribute.

In *The Inspiring Leader* (2009) by leadership executives John H. Zenger, Joseph R. Folkman and Scott K. Edinger the trio point out that the ability to inspire is near the top of any analysis or survey of what people or organizations look for in a leader. They write that inspirational leaders have qualities such as charisma, confidence and vision that can create a hopeful, positive, confident, self-actualizing and resilient corporate culture.

Oh dear! Perhaps this is an element of leadership still more suited to those with high achievement motivation after all.

Yet we should suspend such harsh judgements for a moment. Superior leaders – through their actions, behaviours and attitudes – exemplify what they want from others, state the trio. Team individuals imitate a role model, with the leader being the obvious candidate as long as we behave in a way that deserves imitation. The pace of work, the standard of output, the client-facing culture and the norms of office life are therefore dictated by you, the leader, acting as a role model.

"A leader leads by example, whether he intends to or not," they write.

This makes the notion of inspiration more than simply the ability to stand before an army and persuade it to run towards an enemy machine gun – with the leader at the front. It involves setting appropriate standards and propagating profitable behaviour by our own example. How you work and behave in the workplace, therefore – as well as how you deal with others – is as inspiring as any

Henry V style entreaties to battle. Indeed, a corporate culture that encouraged the army to think of ways of reaching its objective without having to run towards the machine gun would be far more inspiring – especially in the modern world where you are likely to be leading highly educated graduates or highly experienced professionals that simply want the freedom to develop their own skills while learning from an inspiring role model.

Motivating a team

Anthony Robbins (1992) states that most companies motivate their employees using negative reinforcements as their core strategy. This basically means fear, which takes us back to the primary motivation of those with high fear of failure: avoidance. Yet recovering High-FF leaders, more than anyone, should understand how debilitating this is for the worker, as well as how short term and self-defeating for the leader.

The second strategy, according to Robbins, involves financial incentives. He states that this is an excellent idea that is usually appreciated, although he says money as a reward offers diminishing returns, especially with respect to loyalty – as anyone witnessing the rush of resignations on the day the bonuses are paid in the City of London or Wall Street can attest.

"The third and most powerful strategy for motivating people," says Robbins, "is through personal development."

By helping them grow and expand personally – through training and mentoring, through developing their autonomy, through added responsibilities and project management, through bringing them further and further into the strategic and objectives-setting process – you will help your team feel passionate about their jobs and want to contribute more, which is going to make *your* life a whole lot easier.

And if this all feels like a long way from the management you experienced from your own line manager then so much the better.

Your role as a leader is not to ape the failed practices of past leaders, but to promote a better way and be in charge of making that better way happen.

Loyalty runs down the hierarchy, not up

In fact, the point of leadership is that the concept of loyalty runs in totally the opposite direction to that which those with a high fear of failure both think and expect (or most have experienced). We need to become an advocate for the people who report to us – standing up for *them*.

Donald. P Ladew in *How to Supervise People* (1998) states that we should intervene on behalf of our team when someone is threatening their ability to do the job and that we must insist any complaint about the team is handled by us – refusing to allow others to bypass our authority. We must also be their source of stability in times of change, as well as *their* catalyst for self-improvement.

"Great supervisors succeed by leading others to success," he says.

If new to the role Ladew offers some "supervisor basics" such a making yourself known (to the entire team), waiting before making any major changes, and ignoring rumours and gossip. However, you also need to identify the people within your team who make things work, set high goals and be upbeat and positive, although you must accept your role as a supervisor. You don't have to be "one of the gang" nor "be a pal to everyone in order to get them on your side."

Using High-FF traits to our advantage

Yet we must remember that our role as a leader is to inspire, which – astonishingly – should be the easy bit for the recovering High-FF. We can use typical fear of failure traits to our advantage. These include:

Enthusiasm: Our emotional responses are often negatively aligned. Once things are going the right way, however, they can provide emotional support for our team via our genuine and often-overflowing enthusiasm.

Diligence: As stated, High-FFs tend to over-prepare. We rarely "wing it" – making us strong leaders for those looking for an inspirational example to follow.

Empathy: Again, as previously stated, once looking the right way we are capable of great sensitivity towards those we lead – exactly what the modern leader needs to sustain, enthuse and drive his or her team.

Creativity: We are different. We think outside the box. Good for us – once switched towards our positive pursuits (rather than fearful shadows), such creativity will impress and inspire our team.

As Ladew says: "The way you handle the people you supervise is one of the largest factors in your success of failure as a supervisor" – or, come to that, your success or failure as a recovering High-FF.

Case Study 16 – The "impostor"

Christine is the head of a well-known charity – an important job that carries great responsibility. Yet she wrote to me saying she suffered from severe doubts about her ability to lead.

"I sit in important meetings and feel like an impostor," she wrote. "It's as if someone is going to tap me on the shoulder and say – 'you can't do this can you?' I wait for the moment I'm rumbled, despite the fact I've worked in this sector for many years and had previous experience as a director of another large charity."

Of course, she was well aware that "impostor phenomenon" was a common concern – especially among female executives. Yet such knowledge offered her only limited comfort.

"It's the impact on my judgement that's the key issue," she said. "It's not that I assume everyone's out to get me. But I do think I'm not rated by my team, and that has a corrosive impact on my abilities. I get into unnecessary conflicts with colleagues."

Impostor phenomenon was first observed by psychologists Pauline Clance and Suzanne Imes and described in their 1978 paper *The Impostor Phenomenon Among High Achieving Women* (they shy away from calling it a "syndrome," which is more a media tag).

"They consider themselves to be 'impostors'," they write, ". . . believing that they are really not bright and have fooled anyone who thinks otherwise. Numerous achievements, which one might expect to provide ample objective evidence of superior intellectual functioning, do not appear to affect the impostor belief."

And while the phenomenon was discovered in professional women, it can impact anyone who sits at a table of apparent peers yet feels insecure at that table despite having earned their place.

For Christine, however, it was especially painful.

"I work in a sector where we are supportive by definition," said Christine. "But here am I feeling constantly under attack, which makes me think the worst of people. I end up being a backstabber. Of course, I hate myself for it, but the second there's some negative gossip about someone else, I feel better about myself. It's horrible."

She ended by saying that reading *What's Stopping You?* had prompted her to reread Dale Carnegie, and she was now "actively suppressing" her criticisms of others.

"I find if I support others, they support me: at least, that's the theory," she wrote – ending her note with a smiley face.

What's Stopping You? *Your potential as a leader is enormously strengthened if you can remember that the experiences you felt on the way up are being felt by those you now lead. You should delegate effectively, be a strong mentor and praise liberally. You should also be a bold and imaginative recruiter, despite your High-FF instincts.*

PART FIVE
Me Inc.

17

THE HIGH-FF ENTREPRENEUR

How's this for a question at the back end of the book: could someone with a high fear of failure become an entrepreneur – creating and running his or her own business? Or could they perhaps become a freelancer – relying on their own skills and attributes to hunt and execute work for their own account?

Working for yourself is probably the greatest leap you could make in terms of taking responsibility for your own destiny. It is also the ultimate move in depersonalization – taking *Me Inc.* to its logical conclusion.

We will deal with freelancing below. Meanwhile, we should consider starting a business – not least because many High-FFs avoid entrepreneurship. Undoubtedly, some will have been scared off by all that "start your own business" literature, which suggests that the stereotypical image of a successful entrepreneur is a million miles from the personality of those with a high fear of failure. Take this description from British entrepreneurial guru Mike Southon in his well-known business start-up guide *The Beermat Entrepreneur* (written with Chris West in 2002):

"Entrepreneurs are confident. They are born optimists: they simply *know* they can do it . . . Entrepreneurs are also charismatic. They inspire people . . . they have optimism to spare which they radiate and instil into others around them . . . Entrepreneurs are ambitious . . . Entrepreneurs are in a hurry . . . Entrepreneurs are also arrogant. They know they are good. At everything . . . Entrepreneurs are also manipulative . . . Entrepreneurs use people."

Southon is not alone. Entrepreneurial consultants and authors Joseph H. Boyett and Jimmie T. Boyett come to a similar conclusion in *The Guru Guide to Entrepreneurship* (2002).

"Successful entrepreneurs are the eternal optimists . . . Successful entrepreneurs are not afraid to make leaps . . . Entrepreneurs respond to the negativism they meet by becoming even more committed to their idea – more convinced they are right."

Virtually all start-up business books conjure the image of an entrepreneur as a swashbuckling risk taker – a confident visionary defying the odds and facing danger with a wink, a whistle and a cheeky grin. Yet these books are of little use to the High-FF because they are focusing on a different audience. Southon is a successful multi-millionaire entrepreneur. And in the passages above he is describing himself (an opinion I can back up from meeting him on several occasions). *The Guru Guide . . .* is similar, citing "natural leaders" willing to make "leaps" including the founders of *Microsoft, Netscape, Disney, Home Depot, Ben & Jerry's Ice Cream, Virgin Group, Dell Computers* and *Amazon* to name just a few.

Both books are focused on the giants and wannabe giants – examining them for clues to becoming a trailblazing entrepreneur of the Sam Walton or Richard Branson stripe. Yet in my opinion the vast majority of entrepreneurs are not like that. Most entrepreneurs are normal people that wanted to work for themselves – either as freelancers or by employing people to help them execute.

These people are far from superhuman – many are, indeed, fearful of the downside risk of working for themselves. Yet many will have become frustrated by their lack of progress in the workplace – perhaps losing out to those that possess the confidence, guile and determination to dominate formal hierarchies. Others will feel that there is prejudice against them so that they are unlikely to prosper within a large organization filled with "people like us" (with them the outsiders).

The entrepreneurial myth

A better perspective comes from small-business guru Michael Gerber's important book on why most small businesses fail called *The E-Myth Revisited* (2004). Referring to the "entrepreneurial myth," Gerber states that people start businesses for many reasons, although most businesses are not started by visionary entrepreneurs but by bookkeepers, barbers, plumbers, salespeople and secretaries who grew tired of working for somebody else.

"Great businesses are not built by extraordinary people but by ordinary people doing extraordinary things," says Gerber.

Another strong book on this subject is *Never Bet the Farm* (2006) by US entrepreneurs Anthony Iaquinto and Stephen Spinelli Jr. They also de-myth the heroic entrepreneur, stating that start-up business people are just ordinary people with fears and faults like everyone else.

Indeed, a key proposition of *Never Bet the Farm* is to be realistic, stating that successful entrepreneurs are "risk managers, not risk takers."

"You should never get comfortable with fear, nor should you try to conquer or ignore it," they state – interestingly citing both *Wal-Mart*'s Sam Walton and *Virgin*'s Richard Branson as two among many who overcame fear-related handicaps to achieve their goals.

And closer to home there's Rachel Bridge, *The Sunday Times* Enterprise Editor. Many of her interviews with British entrepreneurs from all walks of life have made it into several books, including *How I Made It* (2005). In the introduction she describes the typical entrepreneur, or rather she doesn't as she states that entrepreneurs come in all shapes and sizes – "they can be old and young, well educated or not, male or female, naturally confident or painfully shy." She also states that they can be the type of person that "dreams up a dozen new business ideas a day or the sort who has only ever had one – which may not even be original."

"What makes the whole idea of becoming a successful entrepreneur so very exciting," she concludes, "is that there are no rules."

My own experience backs this up. At the height of the dotcom boom, I co-founded and became CEO of *Metrocube*, an "e-business" incubator that leased two no-frills office blocks on the trendy fringes of London's financial district. We installed state-of-the-art technology with the goal of providing space for young dotcom entrepreneurs – getting them out of their bedrooms and into an environment where they could incubate their enterprises.

Ultimately the bubble burst and most of the young enterprises were carried out in a box. Meanwhile, we broadened our scope to include a diverse range of start-ups – meaning that in the three years of our operation we witnessed, and in many cases helped incubate, over 200 small companies.

Traits for sustainability

As CEO I met every one of these companies as they applied to join the community. I also developed a strong sense regarding each company's potential, or otherwise (and charged more or less deposit accordingly). The aim was to create sustainable enterprises capable of steady growth. If that generated an entity of 10 or so people, then that was seen as a great result. Yet – while the sustainable companies were run by people from all backgrounds and with varying personalities – I couldn't help noticing they tended to have certain traits in common. These were my (totally unscientific) observations:

Clarity – the companies that worked had an obvious business plan, usually involving something that was already happening but where they had a niche or had an improved method of delivery or execution. Sure, the dotcom craziness made evaluations along these lines more difficult but I still learnt to be suspicious when someone couldn't explain it to me in one sentence, or – worse – asked for a flip chart and pen to help me "get my head around it."

Funding – most of the successful companies didn't have any. Virtually all the companies that came through the door showing off about their venture-capital backers with deep pockets were driving at break-neck speed towards a brick wall. They kept talking about "rounds" of funding from ever bigger names, although few materialized. In fact, these were usually the companies demanding an entire floor and then wanting to spend a fortune on partitioning and furniture. Meanwhile, they had no income and were burning through their cash at a breathtaking pace.

Income – the survivors came in many guises but they all had income. Someone, somewhere was paying them for what they did, no matter what the amount. This may seem obvious, but it isn't.

Costs – the successful companies were tight as hell on costs. They hated spending money and would argue me down on every expense. These guys would take the cheapest space we could offer simply to get in the building at minimum expense. They had a survivor's instinct for keeping the costs as low as possible.

Ego – the losers had it in spades. I developed a "bolloxometer" when talking to the CEOs and other cocky seniors. Every time the company seemed to be run by an egomaniac, my bolloxometer started flashing red. These characters were great talkers but had no idea how to nurture a company – and its people – from the ground up. They soon disappeared, usually to something "more scaleable" that they'd "cut me in on" or some other nonsense.

Having said this, egotists are also optimists and virtually every book on starting a business states that optimism is a necessary ingredient, which runs counter to the natural pessimism of the High-FF. Yet again, I disagree. In a lot of cases blind optimists were the maniacs careering over the cliff while the cautious pessimists were the ones pursuing a well-developed plan that had covered most downsides.

Sales – a surprising number of companies had nobody focused on sales, which – for any small company – is suicide. As CEO of *Metrocube*, and for *Moorgate*, I saw and see my key role as sales. If the chief executive is not bringing in clients, he or she is either the office manager, which is an expensive indulgence for a start-up, or no more than a cog in the machine – making themselves vulnerable to the person doing the selling. The exception to this is the consultancy type firms, where the clients are looking for the CEO's expertise – making sales and execution a tough balancing act.

Flexibility – as stated, as *Metrocube* sailed into the dotcom maelstrom we had to broaden our offering to become an incubator for all start ups. This worked because the building's high-tech spec was starting to attract more than the dotcoms. Yet this need for flexibility also worked for the start ups that came through our doors. Many began with grand ideas about online exchanges or online retail operations, for instance, and ended up being software providers for major corporations looking to develop their own internet offering. The CEO usually seemed happy with this – almost relieved – although we noticed the trendier and flakier hangers-on drift off at this point.

Exit – most of the successful companies in *Metrocube* had one eye on "value realization," such as a trade sale to a larger rival. But there were limits to this. Those convinced they would be "IPOing" in six months or so were invariably talking rubbish. However, I noticed that companies with an exit over the horizon, or at least as a long-term goal, tended to have a more professional set-up. That said, companies looking for a short-term sale looked and acted, and in many cases were, fakes – their lack of long-term commitment standing out like a beacon.

Commitment – which brings us to the biggest determinant of them all. It was difficult to tell from the first meeting but within a few weeks it was pretty clear who was committed and who was just having fun or filling in time before college or the consultancy career. Time in the office was a good sign – with those in before eight the clearest winners. Those strolling in past 10 may as well not have bothered (and after a while few of them did).

Oddly, the opposite was true at the other end of the working day. Those staying late into the evening were often disorganized lifestylers not taking it seriously, while those that meant it were gone by eight at the latest. And the all-nighter brigades were also likely to be a flash in the pan. Pool tables, dart boards, fridges full of beer and loud music always made me nervous – all clues that they were playing at it.

I also noticed that commitment was a long way from passion – an emotional fuel that looked easy to conjure in my view, and just as easy to switch in another direction. It was the entrepreneurial equivalent of a one-night-stand – capable of steaming up the windows for a brief but intense moment but hardly what's needed for the long haul. Commitment, meanwhile, was like a marriage. It spoke in measured terms, had a long-term horizon and, as for passion: well that had given way to hard graft and a focus on delivery.

Terror is unavoidable

Sustainable entrepreneuring is, therefore, a long way from the swashbuckling land of heroes often described. It requires hard work over a long period, strong organizational skills and grounded salesmanship. What it does not require is genius or headless bravery or, importantly, uniquely High-AM traits such as over-confidence or blind optimism. Gerber's *E-Myth* . . . concurs with this view, making this an important book for the recovering High-FF entrepreneur. He states that tales of women and men defying all odds to win fame and profit are rarely true and a false god for those pondering a start-up business. The real story is the initial spark of entrepreneurial excitement dissolving into "terror, exhaustion and misunderstanding."

Yet such descriptions should not deter the recovering High-FF – far from it. Terror is our natural state. We should be able to cope with it better than those High-AMs who may truly experience fear for the first time once the support mechanisms of a large organization disappear. Certainly, as an entrepreneur I spend my days in a state of fear – especially in December when our annual PR contracts are renewed (or otherwise). But I spent my days as a banker in fear.

The difference now is that I'm in control. It's fear with the frustration removed. And that is the fear of freedom, which tastes a whole lot sweeter.

Case Study 17 – Edward Stobart, High-FF

Edward Stobart died in March 2011, aged just 56. Yet, despite his ubiquitous trucks on the UK's motorway network, Stobart died as something of an unknown. Even the trucks carry his father's name – Eddie – although it was Edward that turned it into the country's most famous trucking brand.

From the excellent obituary of him in the *Economist*, I think I've worked out why. Unlike his more famous contemporary entrepreneurs – who effuse the confidence and chutzpah and sheer certainty that the image of the entrepreneur (incorrectly) insists is a requirement for success – Edward Stobart, in my view, appeared to suffer from fear of failure.

First of all, he had a stammer, brought about by a traumatic childhood event – in his case a fall through a roof. This appeared to induce the classic fear conditioning in Stobart, who developed his pronounced stammer when in fearful situations such as meeting new people.

And no matter how large the business became, the persona of Eddie Stobart Ltd was through the trucks rather than Edward. Mostly, he was the man eating egg and chips in the lorry-park café, with his fellow diners oblivious to the fact he was by far the most famous name in UK haulage.

Stobart was always polite and always smart, but he shied away from meeting strangers – a trait that prevented a public flotation of the company until after he sold his majority stake to his brother. My guess (and it is only a guess) was that he distrusted financial advisers and shareholders – perhaps fearing that their intrusion, and expertise, would reveal his personally perceived (but deeply held) self-belief in his own inadequacies.

Certainly, trust was an issue for Stobart. As a child he showed entrepreneurial flair but kept all his savings in his trouser pocket. And he forced upon his drivers a rigid dress and conduct code (including wearing ties – something unheard of in the grease-and-nicotine world of trucking). In fact his lack of trust in his workforce went as far as washing many of the trucks himself.

Of course, both the tie-wearing and manual truck-washing may suggest – not distrust – but a strong desire to project an upright professional image in a world renowned for sloppiness and poor manners. Yet such a desire to over-compensate can, of course, be based on perceived insecurities regarding how the world might judge him or his brand.

Indeed, he confessed that a lot of the brand's power was down to image. He "didn't hesitate to lie about how many lorries he had," stated *The Economist* obituary. Again, this could show chutzpah but could equally reveal deeply held feelings of inadequacy – as *The Economist* writes: "With his stammer, it was much easier to say, 'no problem' than to start picking difficulties."

What's Stopping You? *There is no such thing as a "typical" entrepreneur, so don't be put off by the image. All you need is a strong desire to work for yourself, commitment and organization. Yes, you will experience fear, but fear as an entrepreneur is the fear of freedom, which tastes a lot sweeter.*

18

ALTERNATIVE PATHS FOR THE HIGH-FF

Entrepreneurship can be a terrifying experience, even for those with high achievement motivation. For the High-FF it can feel like a leap too far, as well as a move that might destroy our progress – sending us reeling back to our "I'm not good enough" worst after just minor setbacks.

This is partly due to the enormity of the endeavour. Support mechanisms such as publicly sponsored schemes or incubators (such as *Metrocube*) go only so far. Mostly, we are on our own, which can undermine the *Me Inc.* robustness we may have been developing.

Yet there are alternatives to "going it alone," of which the most common is to go into business with a partner. Indeed, partnerships represent a significant milestone for the recovering High-FF capable of mastering them. The thought of running a business as a joint venture with another person (or persons) as equal partners is both enticing – our partner may bring some of the entrepreneurial requirements we still lack (such as confidence, optimism, courage and other traits typical of those with high achievement motivation) – and at the same time concerning. We are likely to harbour typical High-FF concerns regarding trust.

"Partnerships don't work"

Certainly, my own experience with partners has been a bad one. So much so that I spent years adopting the typical entrepreneurial mantra that partnerships don't work, which is patently untrue: there have been as many successful companies built through partnership as there have been by single operators, if not more.

Both *Metrocube* and *Moorgate* were founded as partnerships, although both barely survived the experience. At *Metrocube* my partner put in more money (including family money) and it was his initial spark. Neither he nor I managed to get beyond this, which meant that – despite being CEO – I felt constantly undermined, sometimes even humiliated in front of colleagues. He assumed his greater shareholding (a majority if his friends and family were included) gave him additional authority, and he thought me a little flaky, perhaps assuming I was filling in time between banking and the publication of my first book.

Yet the experience was reversed at *Moorgate*. A journalist and former colleague suggested we team up. Needing a catalyst for my own nascent plans of creating a specialist communications agency for banks, and confirmation from someone with high achievement motivation, I jumped at his offer of a 50:50 partnership, although I provided the majority of the resources – at first using *Metrocube* as an incubator.

My assumption that he would play my former role of full-time executioner in this venture – while I finalized the sale of *Metrocube* and potentially dabbled elsewhere – was, however, flawed. We had very different notions of what it took to start a company, with his eventually angering me, as did his work on other projects (ignoring my own activities in this regard).

Typical High-FF partnership failings

Of course, my reaction to both scenarios was typical of someone with a high fear of failure: frustration, followed by distrust, followed by emotional rather than rational responses. Yet my experiences are poor and, probably, self-fulfilling. Partnerships can be a sound way for businesses to grow, especially if the partners can provide different skills. Partnerships are based on trust, however, and – as with my two examples – if the trust is absent or breaks down they can quickly dissolve into feuding and destructive rivalries.

With both my experiences I felt I was let off lightly, mainly because of the people involved (other than me, that is). Looking back I realize it was my High-FF status that was the main cause of the problems in both cases. My weakness at the start of the relationship translated into distrust during it. This caused me to behave in ways that led them to distrust me (probably correctly), creating – as is so often the case with the High-FF – a self-fulfilling vortex of destruction.

Towards strong partnering

In his book *Let's Go into Business Together* (2001), Azriela Jaffe states strong communication as the "platinum rule" for a successful partnership, which of course sounds obvious until we try and put it into practice. In my case, I was so busy trying to get my own points across – inwardly shouting "listen to me, listen to me" – that I had no time or inclination to listen to them.

Not for the first time, Jaffe compares partnerships to a marriage. He suggests that, like all intimate relationships, partnerships begin with a romantic phase with giant helpings of harmony, compromise and charm. Both partners are trying to look and act in ways the other will find attractive, and the tendency at this stage is to only see the other's attractive qualities. Yet reality inevitably kicks in – perhaps at the first crisis when those warning signals that have been actively ignored start flashing red.

"The honeymoon stage never lasts forever – in marriage or in a business partnership," writes Jaffe. "Power struggles and disenchantment are painful but necessary processes that all intimate relationships pass through."

Jaffe suggests that the romantic phase is the key moment to put in place the foundations for a strong partnership, which include (again, with some of my own thoughts thrown in):

Slow down. Don't rush into partnership. Why not "live together before getting married," suggests Jaffe, meaning first working together on a few projects?

Prepare a pre-nuptial. A partnership agreement is essential. It should state each partner's investment in the venture and commitment to it, as well as other commitments that may get in the way.

Account for strengths and weaknesses. The agreement can include the skills and qualities each brings. This is essential in modern (and more mature) partnerships where individuals actively seek partners from different backgrounds (sales and IT being a typical one) – part of what Jaffe calls the "paradigm shift in partnering" and a far more effective approach than two mates going into business because they got on well at college and had an idea over their third beer.

Introduce the family. Would you introduce your business partner to your mother? If not, why not? You may have the same problem with potential clients.

Prepare a mission statement. Even if a marriage of two established businesses, a new business is being created and that requires a new business plan and, most importantly, a mission statement. The creation of such a statement may shed light on differing objectives and motivations, and – once agreed – the shared goals should help iron out minor disputes.

When partnerships go wrong

Of course, every element above is aimed at breaking the fall when the inevitable "day of disillusionment" arrives, says Jaffe.

This is a key moment for the High-FF, who may have gone into the partnership naively thinking his or her partner provided the props they lacked. Almost certainly, the disillusioned High-FF will focus on a perceived loss of trust – behaviours and actions by the other that have eroded what was probably an untenable level of trust or emotional investment in the first place.

Jaffe states that, at this point, you will probably focus your energies on getting your partner to change, an approach that will quickly have you in your corner – hurling insults and perhaps destroying any potential for salvation. If you instead try and see it from *their* point of view, focusing on how *you* can change (at the very least in terms of your approach), and how you can accommodate their view, you may see them also soften their stance.

Even if you suspect your partner of dishonesty, you should stay honest. Even if you suspect your partner's motives, you should remain frank about yours. And even if you are consumed with anger, you should stay calm – communicating with your partner the way you expect them to communicate with you (my biggest challenge, for sure).

The positive side of partnerships

But this all seems so negative – as if the best result available is gritted tolerance and stale endeavour. Hotel entrepreneur Jonathan M. Tisch rails against such negativity in his book *The Power of We* (written with Karl Weber in 2004) – stating that partnerships offer a different approach to leadership and a strong reaction to the testosterone-fuelled "titans of industry" approach that, he suggests, most often ends in disaster and disgrace.

"The myth of the go-it-alone business hero is just that – a myth," says Tisch.

To prove this, Tisch widens the definition of partnership to embrace clients, suppliers, social agencies, employees and even competitors – not least because it transforms our attitude away from the "me first" ethos. Partnerships at all levels should be equal and based on compromise and commitment, says Tisch. Finding reasons not to cooperate is easy, he says, while finding reasons to cooperate requires creative thought (echoing Carnegie).

Yet this is all very easy to write. For High-FFs at least, such concepts are far more difficult to undertake, especially consistently. Help comes from the great man himself, Stephen Covey, in *The Seven Habits . . .* His sixth habit is "synergize," which he describes as "bringing together a whole that is greater than the sum of the parts." Covey states that synergy is everywhere in nature – even in the way a man and woman bring a child into the world.

"The essence of synergy is to value differences," says Covey. "To respect them, to build on strengths, to compensate for weaknesses."

Yet being effective depends on trust, which can be difficult if we react defensively, or by being authoritarian or even passive. These are reflexive reactions, says Covey, which – as High-FFs well understand – can be disastrous. We may oppose or we may tolerate, but we do not actively cooperate and, according to Covey, cooperation and communication are the two legs of a successful synergistic relationship.

Covey states that truly synergistic relationships – that produce "solutions better than any originally proposed" where all parties "genuinely enjoy the creative enterprise" – are produced from positions of sincere trust: where we have fully and co-operatively invested in the other party.

Again, my own experiences – where the motivations and objectives of my partners were seemingly at odds with my own, making trust impossible – makes me wonder whether Covey is being naïve here, although he covers this eventuality.

"There are some circumstances in which synergy may not be achievable," he says, before adding that – even in these circumstances – we will benefit from the spirit of sincere trying because it means we avoid a damaging intransigence.

And this means we can walk away with a smile, a shrug and an effective compromise, rather than with further confirmation of our insecurities and fears. Certainly, compromise and spiritual generosity – whatever the physical cost – is a whole lot better than digging trenches while nursing feelings of injustice, although – of course – some High-FFs are programmed to prefer it that way.

Freelancing and consultancy work

But partnering is far from the only way of forging your own path. Another option – and one that chimes with the modern economy – is freelancing (if offering your skills) or consulting (if offering your expertise). Certainly, the regulatory burdens of employment have encouraged many larger companies to source skills from independent individuals, rather than keep growing the workforce. And this has led to a growth in the opportunities for freelancers and consultants. For freelancers, this is especially the case in the creative industries (including IT) – and in construction – where projects may be "lumpy": meaning that a large workforce may be a requirement one week and a burden the next. For consultants, professional services companies often contract consultants on particular projects – again because maintaining a team of professionals is expensive when the work being won comes in fits and starts. And many also appreciate an external view when it comes to strategy.

Yet such options are also attractive to the freelancer/consultant. Many freelancers live lifestyles incompatible with corporate life, or are simply not cut out for the discipline of the workplace. Meanwhile, consultants are often professionals nearing retirement who may find commuting (at least in rush-hour) a drag and corporate life somewhat overbearing. Both may have been uncomfortable with the brutality of office politics, or may have felt their contribution was unrecognized within the organization that won their exclusive output – in all cases making freelancing/consulting a strong alternative path.

In Going Solo (1997), William Bond tackles the requirements for growing a successful "home-based" consultancy (i.e. a one-person, skill-based, time-billing business). He states that consultants are in demand in many fields. They also attract good money and win flexible employment arrangements. But you *must* have something to offer, he says, and be able to effectively communicate that offering to your potential audience. His tips for sustainable consulting include (inevitably including my own thoughts):

Create your workspace. Make sure you can work from home. Kitchen-table businesses will soon fail if the table is too regularly invaded by noisy kids, demanding spouses or visiting neighbours. As with "managing the process," you need to set yourself up to succeed. "Your business will [only] be successful when you get the support and cooperation from others within your household," says Bond.

Communicate. Tell everyone you meet what you do. Bond suggests developing your own 30-second "elevator speech" so that people quickly understand your skills and the circumstances of your offering (a 10-second version will be even more effective). Business cards and flyers help. Obscure but clever names for your business do not.

Get marketing. Many freelancers/consultants fail to prosper because they become too dependent on one client – perhaps their former employer. Do some research and make some approaches to likely buyers, or you may soon exhaust your options.

Follow up. "Success results from following up every enquiry and response," says Bond. You are no longer in a corporate environment, so your networking needs to be more urgent and with a stated purpose, which is to win business. Yet don't pester. New contacts can be quickly lost if you become too demanding.

Please. It is far easier to please an existing client than to find a new one – so make sure you deliver. One common mistake for freelancers, in the early days, is to over-charge for unfinished work (thinking that the client is undervaluing their skills). Most corporates are used to this, but it irritates. And they will come back again and again to the person that offers good value and a professional (i.e. reliable, timely and complete) service.

Learn about your client. This is true for targeting clients as well as executing their projects. Distance makes it easy for a freelancer/consultant to miss the brief and take projects in the wrong direction. This is wasteful for the client and can turn positive communication into defensive conflict – all of which could have been avoided by listening carefully to the client. Again, High-FF insecurities can obscure this simple rule – making you more interested in winning praise for *your* "brilliance" than in listening to *their* needs.

Think vertically as well as horizontally. It isn't just about selling your skill-set to the widest number of potential buyers. It's about exploring what you can offer the clients you already have. This is the classic "farmer/hunter" divide in sales, with the farmer (of existing clients) a potentially neglected opportunity. There may be tangential work available for those with a good track-record of client delight. For instance, at *Moorgate* we often employ freelance writers, but one has proven adept at page-layout for newsletters – a skill we can market on her behalf.

The franchising alternative

And then there's franchising – sometimes called "soft entrepreneuring" because much of the hard work of building a brand and marketing its products and services has been done for the franchisee by the franchiser. Some of the world's most famous brands are franchises, with franchisees buying the rights to open an operation and receive marketing and operational support (as well as a famous name) in return. *MacDonalds, Subway, Dunkin Donuts, Pizza Hut, Domino's Pizza, KFC, Prontaprint, 7-eleven, Kwik-Fit, Londis* – all are franchise operations with each branch a separate business owned by the man or woman behind the till (or their manager out back). Even professional services are getting in on the act – with law firm *Baker & McKenzie* operating along franchise lines (making it the second largest law firm in the world).

That said, franchising is an entrepreneurial option that comes with strings attached.

"Franchising is a negotiated relationship in which franchisers and franchisees must live with some degree of flexibility regarding each other's performance," writes Stephen Spinelli Jr (of *Never Bet the Farm* fame), Robert M. Rosenberg and Sue Birley in *Franchising* (2004).

By flexibility, the trio can mean the opposite. For obvious reasons, franchisers are fierce defenders of their brand and reputation. So while some of the entrepreneurial terror is reduced – not least through travelling a well-tested operational path – some of the frustration is not.

This is freedom with limits, although this may actually suit the High-FF entrepreneur. We spend our life scouring the horizon for icebergs – often bailing out at the first white-spec on the horizon (when it was a perfectly navigable obstacle, or even a potential opportunity). So here's a route that comes with a pilot – albeit one we've had to pay for. For the High-FF, that may be a price worth paying.

Developing a mental autonomy

Finally, you should consider the ultimate alternative to running your own business – developing an enterprising attitude within your current workplace. This is perhaps the easiest of the *Me Inc.* recovery steps on offer for the High-FF, although it still requires a complete change in attitude if it's not to be eroded over time. And it does require some support from the organization you work for.

Workplace entrepreneurialism is a big theme for company guru Tom Peters in *In Search of Excellence*. He implores companies to "atomize" an organization in order to "induce zest, creativity, and . . . symbiosis with the customer." A key part of this, according to Peters, is "entrepreneurizing every job" – making each employee a businessperson with the mindset of the independent contractor.

"Businesses, in order to compete, have to be not just decentralized but deorganized," writes Peters. "The logical limit of deorganization is the entrepreneur – the business unit of one."

What's required, he insists, is a focus on individual proactivity. And while his philosophy is obviously trying to influence managers, in *Thriving on Chaos*, his influential 1987 follow-up to *In Search of Excellence*, he offers attitudes and values that every employee should adopt, no matter what the over-riding culture of the corporation. These include an obsession with service and responsiveness to customers (including serving those we report to); the creation of new ways to organize yourself and to measure your progress (perhaps via strong "customer" feedback); the sourcing of partnerships in every direction (above, below, with colleagues, externally); and the removal of office paranoia by developing transferable skills.

"Be ready to change everything," says Peters. We should embrace the "love of change."

And if you cannot find this much room for manoeuvre within your current organization – move to one where you can. Indeed, this is an important final point for those recovering from fear of failure in their career pursuits. Many High-FFs will have found employment within an organization that shares their previous intolerance of failure – perhaps because of the level of external scrutiny upon it (by regulators, shareholders or – if within the public sector – voters, politicians and the media). As someone soaked in your own fears, this may have been a comforting place to work. But as someone recovering from such insecurities, it may – in fact should – frustrate you, making your next move one to an entrepreneurial organization no matter what its purpose or ownership structure.

Case Study 18 – New routes to advocating franchising

Patrick wrote to me because he thought I could help him with his new venture, but – when we met – we soon found common ground in terms of fears and insecurities and how these had impacted our motivation.

Franchising was Patrick's thing. He'd been introduced to the world of franchising by his parents, who'd become commercial cleaning franchisees as a response to his father's redundancy. Certainly, Patrick was happy working in the family business, although – after several years – was keen to branch out on his own: becoming a franchisee in a specialist area of industrial decontamination.

"There was no pressure on me to become a franchisee," he said, "it just felt like the right thing to do. I was ambitious and could see that it worked. And I could see my parents enjoy it and prosper. But I was motivated to go one better than mum and dad."

As the business took off, however, Patrick developed anxieties. Becoming overly concerned about minor details, he felt unable to delegate and therefore took all the administrative work upon himself, and even some of the boots and overalls work.

"It was *all* on my shoulders," he said, "and my health suffered as a result."

Sleeping poorly, he developed night-sweats and eventually became so anxious about his company he had trouble leaving the house.

After psychological treatment, and some serious thinking time, Patrick decided he'd perhaps developed the wrong goals due to the subconscious influence of his parents – and their success in franchising. Employing people and winning and executing large contracts was less appealing to Patrick than the concept of franchising as an entrepreneurial route, which led him to develop a role as a franchising consultant to people considering this form of business ownership.

"Once I looked at what really motivated me, I could see that I was an advocate of the model, but that didn't mean that I had to become a franchisee," he said. "Certainly, I can tell whether people are ready for franchising or not, and – if so – what area they should research, as well as how different routes compare to their own goals and ambitions. It's my knowledge and experience I'm offering, which I can use to help others."

What's Stopping You? *Starting a new business can be a lonely affair, which will increase the terror. And while partnerships, freelancing/consultancy and even franchising come with frustrations, all offer positive and less terrifying entrepreneurial routes for the High-FF. That said, entrepreneurship is an attitude that High-FFs can adopt no matter where they work.*

CONCLUSION – THE POINT OF RECOVERY

This book began with a healthy dose of scepticism towards the self-help industry. And, having stripped it bare of its useful tips and advice, it should conclude the same way. The modern self-help industry is just that: an industry. It has inputs (insecure people like us) and outputs (books and DVDs and lecture tours and surgeries and TV shows and even the odd gizmo). And it has a process: focusing the mind of the input on his or her own happiness and/or fulfilment and/or potential.

As Stephen Covey points out, it has also changed with the times: moving from a 19th-century focus on character building, in which virtues such as hard work and efficiency were promoted, to a thoroughly modern obsession with quick-fix techniques that "cure" our insecurities (in "under an hour") and bring us instant success, constant happiness and dream fulfilment.

In an age where we want it all *now*, an industry has sprung up to tell us we can instantly have it all – *well, there's a surprise*!

So is my job to tell you that this is impossible? Not really, as even the most avid devourer of the genre is aware of the over-promising of the "dream fulfilment" gurus (although they may still be vulnerable to the promise of a "cure" for their insecurities when, as most psychologists point out, we are hardwired to our inner beliefs). My job has been to try and marry the two – to accept the science, and the monkey as a constant if annoying companion, but to enlist the gurus and gizmos where they are useful for our progress. To try and offer a route for progress despite our inner beliefs – not to offer a rewiring where rewiring is impossible.

In fact, I contend that many of the gurus would quietly accept the charge of over-promising, defending it on those classic grounds that, if we aim high, we'll land higher than if we aim midway, even if we land lower than the stated objective. This is fine for goal-setting, although obviously contradicts many claims regarding constant happiness (constant frustration, more like). But it is absolutely not fine when tackling psychological conditions such as fear of failure. As stated, self-denial – however deeply held and effectively masked – is no cure. It is a delayed reckoning.

Quit obsessing

Yet this is a long way from a depressing conclusion. It is a treatise for acceptance, one that states that I am who I am, and now let's tackle the future. Although even here we have to be careful. Obsessing about anything – the past, the future, us, them – is unhealthy and can steer us down a dark path to nowhere.

Certainly, this is the contention of psychologist Paul Pearsall in his attack on the self-help industry called *The Last Self-Help Book You'll Ever Need* (2005). Self-absorption, says Pearsall, can magnify your problems until they feel unmanageable. Pearsall's contention is that there is "not just one good life" so you should stop looking for it and look for "*a* good life" instead. His view is that discontentment cannot be cured by consumption, even of ideas. As an alternative, he suggests you pursue his "seven attributes" of a healthy personality:

- Be sceptical, especially of books that distil life's wisdom into a few rules.
- Deceiving yourself about others can be in your interest – especially in a marriage.
- Embrace the craziness of your family.

- Workaholism is not bad for you if you are doing what you love.
- Obsessing about health is bad for your health.
- It is impossible to stay young forever, so enjoy the moment.
- Death is just another part of life.

Be self-critical

You cannot have a positive attitude all the time, states Pearsall, who openly questions the idea of clinging to high self-regard no matter what the setback – therefore reducing your ability to be self-critical. Guilt and shame are not always the villains, self-esteem not the only "sacred cow." Doubt, depression, guilt, even shame can spur people to change for the better, he says, while hope and positivity can wrap people so tightly in their future goals that they miss the present moment.

Instead of self-improvement you should choose a different goal, says Pearsall: enjoying your life. You should therefore savour the present – even the bad bits – instead of seeking happiness in the future.

"There isn't anything wrong with being depressed," says Pearsall. "Life and its transitions can be sad. Crying . . . is not being 'dysfunctional'. It's being human."

In defence of melancholy

English professor Eric G. Wilson takes this a stage further in his book *Against Happiness* (2008) in which he defends melancholy as a condition. Few people accept a melancholic mood as a potentially beneficial state of mind and the entire self-help industry seems to be geared towards its banishment. Yet Wilson contends that sadness "sparks grand thought, sublime inspiration and vital creativity," prompting people to "turn away from superficiality and to look deeper into the meaning of things."

"Melancholia is the profane ground out of which springs the sacred," is his rather florid take on it (he is an English professor after all), adding that such lows keep the "mind questing, questioning and alive."

Those that strive for unending happiness, says Wilson, are essentially seeking control. And it is often the lack of control – the feeling of powerlessness – that most concerns the insecure. Yet Wilson quotes philosopher Alan Watts who states that "there is a contradiction in wanting to be perfectly secure in a universe whose very nature is momentariness and fluidity."

Constant happiness is therefore an artificial state, says Wilson, and its pursuit a religion with its own high priests (the motivational gurus) who fuel a hopeless drive to tame a future that is – of course – untameable.

Stephen Covey agrees: "To think we are in control is an illusion," he says in *First Things First* (written in 1994 with Roger and Rebecca Merrill). "It puts us in a position of trying to manage consequences."

Covey's view is that any paradigm based on control – of time, people or consequences – is bound to fail, so it is pointless to base our happiness on such a quest.

Choosing to serve

So what should the recovering High-FF seek – especially once we have mastered (or at least understood) our emotions and set in place long-term objectives and a plan for achieving them? Again, Covey has the answer.

"Choosing to serve becomes the most enlightened habit of all," he writes in *The 8th Habit* (2004).

Don't worry, I'm not about to get all touchy-feely in the final analysis. Covey's very practical advice states that once we stop looking inward and, instead, start looking outward we are on the path to what he calls "enlightenment" but what I would rather call "sustainable recovery." It might just be the case that the most debilitating High-FF trait of all is self-obsession. And that the most effective counter is the exact opposite – a concern for the other person. Covey's eighth habit, therefore, focuses on "finding your voice and helping others find theirs." Voice, in this context, is your "unique personal significance" – the key element of yourself that you can offer others (without becoming the preaching motivational convert, I hasten to add).

I have noticed this at Moorgate. The element of the job that gives me most satisfaction, that has me inwardly punching the air with self-confirmation, is in harnessing the latent writing power of our new employees. When writing my first book I discovered in Strand Books (the famous second-hand bookstore in New York) a book that was unknown in the UK called *On Writing Well* by William Zinsser (first published in 1976). His practical guide for writing non-fiction – along with his clarity and sincerity and sheer passion for the subject – not only transformed my own writing but stirred in me a desire to pass on his teachings, and some of my own. I became evangelical about good writing on even the driest of subjects (and, boy, do we deal with some dry subjects at Moorgate!).

Certainly, I measure the success of Moorgate as much by our ability to turn out strong copywriters as by our ability to attract new clients or add more zeroes to the bottom line. For instance, one unhappy worker left with the parting shot that his only regret was not having learnt to write so well at Oxford while struggling with his English dissertation. Another satisfied customer, in other words.

Empower others

So why should you empower others to find their voice? Well, Covey suggests you consider the alternatives. You could try to lead through control, although that is rarely satisfactory and a recipe for conflict, as many High-FFs have discovered. Or you could abdicate responsibility when dealing with people, which may well have been your strategy thus far with obviously unsatisfactory results for your progress. The third – and only sustainable – option, according to Covey, is to help others achieve *their* goals, making that a primary concern in *your* endeavours.

You should help others calculate their own long-term objectives and then set about aiding their achievement, opines Covey. If you do this genuinely – meaning that you are not simply recruiting them for your own goal pursuits or trying to neutralize their attack on you – you can create "win–win" empowerment: the idea that your own progress is bound together with the progress of those you encounter, whether this is at work, at home or even in your social life.

This is a fantastically enlightening concept for those with a high fear of failure, in my opinion. Through binding our goals with those of others we have immediately reduced a damaging self-absorption, which puts us in the right frame of mind to radically improve our people skills. We have also unlocked the positive traits that, as we have seen, High-FFs possess in abundance. Our innate creativity and sensitivity, and our strong potential for leadership, can be positively and fearlessly employed because the result is not about us, it's about them. And by depersonalizing our pursuits the monkey is sidelined, or at least more easily dismissed, because he has no domain over other people.

So far from turning us into overly worthy sandal-wearing do-gooders, helping others achieve their goals may prove to be the High-FF's most powerful and liberating tool for recovery.

Case Study 19 – Giving too much

Shazia came to one of my fear of failure evenings. She hung back after the event, quietly waiting over half an hour for her turn to talk to me. I could see she was uncomfortable with aspects of what I'd been saying throughout the talk, but it was the final element – on "finding your unique gift and offering it to others" – that was the killer for Shazia. And she struggled through her fragile emotional state to tell me why.

"I already give too much," she said, having to measure her speech and tighten her throat in order to keep her emotions under control. "That's my problem. That's what I do. I spend my entire life giving. I help others so much that I never help myself. That's why I came tonight. I want to do something for myself, not others. Give, give, give – that's all I do."

This floored me for a second. Of course, a classic fear of failure trait – especially in women – is to assume the role of the giver and end up becoming both an emotional and physical doormat. And, of course, such an outcome will undermine rather than build confidence, as well as generate resentments. Like the Box 2 interruptions of Covey's activity-grid, it smothers proactivity and goal-oriented pursuits with its sheer urgency.

After a moment's thought, I offered an opinion.

"It sounds like you are giving your time and energy to others but not your unique gift," I ventured. "In fact your unique gift stays hidden – suppressed even."

I asked her what she'd been most proud of – what had given her that great sense of whopping achievement. She hesitated before telling me it was teaching her mother to speak English, which had given her mother enormous confidence.

"Seeing her talk to shopkeepers in English was a fantastic thrill," she said.

Now smiling, she said "thank you," and left. And a week or so later I received an email informing me she'd enrolled on a TEFL (teaching English as a foreign-language) course with the intention of using her skills in both London and Bangladesh, which was a pretty self-reaffirming outcome for both of us.

What's Stopping You? *Obsessing about anything, including ourselves, is unhealthy and can magnify our problems. Helping others achieve their goals is a strong alternative for the recovering High-FF – not least because the monkey has no domain over other people.*

Step One: Discover your *true values*

Visualizing your goals could lead you in the wrong direction without first establishing your *true values*.

- Research your values across a long-enough timeframe to span different moods and needs (for example, Sunday family get-together, Monday meeting, Friday socializing, etc.).
- Focus on discovering what is truly important to *you*: health, intellect, friendship, family, success, etc.
- Also ask *why*? The *why* answers provide a firmer foundation for the resulting document: *Your Constitution* – the creation of which is your core concern for Step One.
- *Your Constitution* should be a bullet-pointed statement about what *you* stand for. There are no limits on the number of points, and there should be no material or personal specifics in terms of goals (these come later).
- Make sure *Your Constitution* appeals to your values while being flexible. For example, a statement such as "I want to run a 200-person law firm serving major corporations" is too specific while "I want to combine my professional qualifications

with my entrepreneurial instincts," is more focused on our values and more flexible.

- Once edited, write *Your Constitution* in the back of your day-per-page diary and – importantly – renew it annually. This does not mean a wholesale rewriting but the acceptance that your values are likely to evolve over time.

Step Two: Visualize your goals

With your *true values* established, you should indulge yourself in this most enjoyable of exercises: visualizing yourself 10 years hence.

- Find somewhere alone and away from distractions. Make yourself comfortable. Close your eyes. And travel into your future – projecting yourself forward a full 10 years.
- Examine every detail of your life in 10 years' time. What are you wearing, where are you living, what constitutes work – and play – and who are you with?
- Work should be a key focus. What does your place of work look like: a corner office in a corporate skyscraper, a book-lined study at home, or perhaps a workshop or studio? And where is it: Mayfair, the Cotswolds, Manhattan?
- How do you spend your day: on what projects and with whom? What do the results of your endeavours look like?
- Try focusing on different aspects (work, home, people) at different times – building a detailed picture of the life you want to live 10 years from now.
- Once done, write it all down (writing the final version in the back of your diary). Be specific and describe your life in detail and using present-tense language. "Year 10: I am living in a thatched cottage in Dorset with my wife, two children and two dogs." The more detail the better.

- Make sure your visualized future dovetails with *Your Constitution*. For instance, if you wrote "I want to be a valued part of a thriving community" as part of *Your Constitution* and then visualized yourself living as a hermit in the Outer Hebrides, you may need to reconcile these apparent contradictions.
- Renew your 10-year visualization annually, as you change diaries.

Step Three: Develop the milestones

Now build your path towards that idealized 10-year peak. Divide up the expanse of time in front of you – repeating the visualization exercise for different moments along your timeline.

- To make the 10-year goal achievable, what has to be in place at the halfway stage? Perhaps you wanted four children. Well, number one should be here by year five, perhaps with number two on the way. Meanwhile, being CEO of a multi-national company may mean you should at least work there, or at a rival, and be making progress up the ladder.
- Details are still important: the house, the office, the people, the car. Visualize them all for the five-year stage, and write them down.
- After your year-five visualization, think about year two. Where must you be in 24 months to make the five-year goal not only possible but inevitable? Again, details please.
- Then look at the one-year horizon. What has to be in place in 12 months to make sure you achieve your 24-month goals? Then six months. Then three months. Then one month. Then one week. And then tomorrow. What must you do tomorrow to make sure your one-week goal is achievable?
- When writing the milestones, ignore the "dreaded hows." Only for the immediate steps do you need any focus on *how* something is to be achieved.

Step Four: Establish a strategy and some tactics

Develop a strategy that acts as a bridge between your goals and your tactics – making sure your action points are focused on your objectives.

- Undertake a SWOT exercise in which you divide your current circumstances into *Strengths, Weaknesses, Opportunities* and *Threats* (again, a written exercise for the back pages of your diary).
- Examine the SWOT to calculate a strategy for execution – perhaps focusing on the opportunities and your strengths to guide your early actions and on overcoming your weaknesses as part of a mid-term plan.
- Aim every action point at moving you towards your goals. Arrange them in a linear form (i.e. one after the other), although some flexibility in execution is important (perhaps being deadline driven).
- As with *Your Constitution* and 10-year visualization, the SWOT can be renewed annually, as progress will add strengths but raise different weaknesses, as well as reveal new threats and opportunities – each driving new strategies and tactics.

Step Five: Execute efficiently

Set yourself up for efficiency – and then follow through by turning this process into a habit.

- Invest in your workspace. Buy lots of new stationery and equipment to create an office or workshop you are proud of and want to occupy.
- Divide your week into hourly slots from eight to eight and make the best use of every one of those 84 hours – making sure your

every action is moving you towards your goals. Treat every minute, every hour and certainly every day with this in mind.

- Adopt Stephen Covey's (slightly altered) four-box grid for your every action – noting what actions occupy which of his four boxes: *urgent and important, urgent but not important, not urgent but important* and *not urgent and not important.*

- The *not urgent but important* box is the most important zone for your progress. Work out what is in this box and timetable the hours required to ensure those actions are executed. Make this the centre of your world.

- Meanwhile, *urgent but not important* items are the most distracting and need to be managed. Timetable periods for dealing with these actions and be proactive with those that add distractions (perhaps pre-empting their needs).

- With efficiency gained, you can reframe the *not urgent and not important* actions as the moments you recharge your batteries, connect with significant others and note your progress.

Step Six: Deal with people

There's no progress without improving your people skills.

- Develop a depersonalization of your pursuits. Long-term objectives and an achievable strategy should allow you to become *Me Inc.* or *Me Ltd* – a single-person company pursuing *its* objectives.

- Treat setbacks as strong lessons for future judgements and actions. They are not final judgements upon *you* – just bends in the road for *Me Inc.* as *it* pursues *its* objectives.

- "Develop your compassion." Poor self-beliefs may have given you poor evaluation skills with people. You dislike yourself, so you dislike others and therefore develop low empathy and zero compassion. Reverse this by developing a more compassionate and generous view of all those you encounter.

- Develop win–win strategies with everybody. High-FFs have a poor track-record with win–lose battles – so avoid them. Meanwhile, helping others achieve their victories is immediately sustainable and self-reaffirming.

Step Seven: Find your unique gift

Everyone has something they can offer others. Finding it and focusing on that as an objective is highly effective.

- Spend time discovering your *unique gift*. *Your Constitution* is likely to offer clues, as are your objectives, although it may be something you move towards, rather than adopt immediately.
- Help others calculate *their* long-term objectives and develop strategies for *their* success. This will put you on the road to recovery because you are facing the right way for developing effective people skills.
- Bind your goals with those of others to reduce your own damaging self-absorption. This will also unlock your positive traits, and help neutralize the monkey because he has no domain over other people.

BIBLIOGRAPHY

Agness, Lindsey. *Change Your Life with NLP*. Harlow, UK: Prentice Hall Life, 2008.

Allen, David. *Getting Things Done*. New York: Penguin Group (USA), 2001.

Allen, Roger E. and Allen, Stephen D. *Winnie the Pooh on Success*. London: Dutton Signet/Penguin Putnam, 1997.

Arden, Paul. *It's Not How Good You Are It's How Good You Want To Be*. London: Phaidon, 2003.

Atkinson, J. W. and Litwin, G. H. Achievement motive and test anxiety, conceived as a motive to approach success and to avoid failure. Washington DC: *Journal of Abnormal and Social Psychology*, 1960.

Bates, Tony. *Understanding and Overcoming Depression*. Freedom, CA: Crossing Press, 2001.

Bay, Tom and Macpherson, David. *Change Your Attitude*. Franklin Lakes, NJ: Career Press, 1998.

Bayley, Stephen and Mavity, Roger. *Life's a Pitch*. London: Bantam Press, 2007.

Beckett, Samuel. *Nohow On*. New York: Grove Press, 1996.

Belding, Shaun. *Dealing with the Boss from Hell*. London: Kogan Page, 2005.

Bettger, Frank. *How I Raised Myself From Failure to Success in Selling*. Englewood Cliffs, NJ: Prentice Hall, 1947.

Blanchard, Ken. *One-Minute Manager*. London: HarperCollins, 1983.

Bridge, Rachel. *How I Made It*. London: Kogan Page, 2005.

Brown, Judson. S. Problems presented by the concept of acquired drives (1953), reproduced by D. Bindraand J. Stewart (Eds) in *Motivation: Selected Readings*. London: Penguin, 1966.

Brown, Judson S. Gradients of approach and avoidance responses and their relation to level of motivation. Washington DC: *Journal of Comparative and Physiological Psychology*, 1948.

Boyett, Joseph H. and Boyett, Jimmie T. *The Guru Guide to Entrepreneurship*. Hoboken, NJ: John Wiley & Sons Inc., 2000.

Bond, William J. *Going Solo*. New York: McGraw-Hill, 1997

Cairo, Jim. *Motivation and Goal-Setting*. Franklin Lakes, NJ: Career Press, 1998.

Carlson, Richard. *Don't Sweat the Small Stuff*. London: Hodder & Stoughton, 1988.

Carlson, Richard. *Don't Sweat the Small Stuff at Work*. London: Hyperion, 1998.

Carnegie, Dale. *How to Win Friends and Influence People*. New York: Simon & Schuster, 1936.

Carnegie, Dale. *How to Stop Worrying and Start Living*. New York: Pocket Books, 1948.

Caunt, John. *Boost Your Self Esteem*. London: Kogan Page, 2003.

Chandler, Steve. *Reinventing Yourself*. Franklin Lakes, NJ: Career Press 1998.

Chandler, Steve. *100 Ways to Motivate Yourself*. Franklin Lakes, NJ: Career Press, 2001.

Charney, Dennis. *Discovering Ourselves: The science of emotion – understanding PTSD*. Washington DC: Library of Congress (website).

Clance, Pauline Rose and Imes, Suzanne. The impostor phenomenon in high achieving women. London: *Psychotherapy Theory, Research and Practice (journal)*, 1978.

Covey, Stephen. *Seven Habits of Highly Effective People*. New York: Simon & Schuster, 1989.

Covey, Stephen. *First Things First*. New York: Simon & Schuster, 1994.

Covey, Stephen. *The 8th Habit*. New York: Simon & Schuster, 2004.

Cox, Allen. *Your Inner CEO*. Franklin Lakes, NJ: Career Press, 2007.

Daniell, Mark. *Elements of Strategy*. Hampshire, UK: Palgrave Macmillan, 2006.

de Botton, Alain. *Status Anxiety*. London: Hamish Hamilton, 2004.

DeLuca, Fred. *Start Small, Finish Big*. New York: Warner Business Books, 2000.

Denning, Stephen. *The Secret Language of Leadership*. San Francisco: Jossey-Bass, 2007.

Dooley, Mike. *Notes from the Universe*. Nashville, TN: Totally Unique Thoughts, 2007.

Dweck, Carol. S and Leggett, Ellen L. A social-cognitive approach to motivation and personality. *Psychological Review*. Washington DC: American Psychological Association, 1988.

Evans, Dylan. *Emotion: the Science of Sentiment*. Oxford, UK: Oxford University Press, 2001.

Evans, Phil. *Motivation*. London: Methuen & Co Ltd, 1975.

Favaro, Peter. *Anger Management*. Franklin Lakes, NJ: New Page Books, 2005.

Feather, N. T. The relationship of persistence at a task to expectation of success and achievement related motives. *Journal of Abnormal and Social Psychology*. Washington DC: American Psychological Association, 1961.

Foster, Jack. *How to Get Ideas*. San Francisco: Berrett-Koehler, 1996.

Freud, Sigmund. *Group Psychology and the Analysis of the Ego*. New York: Boni and Liveright, 1922.

Gerber, Michael. *The E-Myth Revisited*. New York: HarperCollins, 2004.

Gladwell, Malcolm. *Outliers*, New York: Little Brown & Co, 2008

Goldsmith, Barton. *Emotional Fitness at Work*. Franklin Lakes, NJ: Career Press, 2009.

Goldsmith, Marshall with Reiter, Mark. *What Got You Here Won't Get You There*. New York: Hyperion, 2008.

Goleman, Daniel. *Emotional Intelligence*. London: Bloomsbury, 1994.

Goleman, Daniel. *Working with Emotional Intelligence*. London: Bloomsbury, 1998.

Griessman, B. Eugene. *Time Tactics of Very Successful People*. New York: McGraw Hill, 1994.

Harvard Business School. *Strategy*. Cambridge, MA: Harvard Business Essentials, 2005.

Heap, Matthew and Adler, Harry. *Handbook of NLP: A Manual for Professional Communications*. Aldershot, UK: Gower, 2002.

Hill, Napoleon. *Think and Grow Rich*. Meriden, CT: The Ralston Society, 1937.

Iaquinto, Anthony and Spinelli Jr, Stephen. *Never Bet the Farm*. San Francisco: Jossey-Bass, 2006.

Jaffe, Azriela. *Let's Go Into Business Together*. Franklin Lakes, NJ: Career Press, 2001.

James, Oliver. *They F*** You Up*. London: Bloomsbury, 2002.

Jeffers, Susan. *Feel the Fear and Do It Anyway*. New York: Fawcett Columbine, 1987.

Jones, Carol D. *Overcoming Anger*, Holbrook, MA: Adams Media, 2004.

Kaplan, Robert S. and Norton, David P. *The Execution Premium*. Cambridge MA: Harvard Business School Publishing, 2008.

Kelsey, Robert. *The Pursuit of Happiness*. London: Bantam Press, 2000.

Kayes, D. Christopher. *Destructive Goal Pursuit*. New York: Palgrave Macmillan, 2006.

Kets de Vries, Manfred. *The Leadership Mystique*. Harlow, UK: FT Prentice Hall, 2001.

Koch, Richard. *Living the 80/20 Way*. London: Nicholas Brealey Publishing, 2005.

Kranz, Gene. *Failure is Not an Option*. New York: Simon & Schuster, 2001.

Ladew, Donald. P. *How to Supervise People*. Franklin Lakes, NJ: Career Press, 1998.

Lakhani, Dave. *The Power of an Hour*. Hoboken, NJ: John Wiley & Sons Inc., 2006.

Lukaszewski, James. *Why Should the Boss Listen to You?* San Francisco: Jossey-Bass, 2008.

MacKenzie, Alec. *The Time Trap*. New York: McGraw Hill, 1972.

Maslow, Abraham. A Theory of Human Motivation. *Psychological Review*. Washington DC: American Psychological Association, 1943.

McClelland, David C. and Atkinson, John W. (Eds) *Methods of Measuring Human Motivation: The Achieving Society*. Princeton, NJ: D. Van Nostrand, 1961.

McClelland, David C., Atkinson, John W. et al. *The Achievement Motive*. New York: Irvington Publishers, 1976.

McCormack, Mark. *What They Don't Teach You at Harvard Business School*. London: Profile Books, 1984.

McGraw, Phillip C. *Life Strategies*. New York: Hyperion, 1999.

Meyer, Paul J. *Attitude & Motivation Volume 2 – Attitude is Everything!* Waco, TX: PJM Resources, 2003.

Michaelson, Steven W. *Sun Tzu for Execution*. Holbrook, MA: Adams Media, 2007.

Miller, N. E. Studies of fear as an acquirable drive. *Journal of Experimental Psychology*. Washington DC: American Psychological Association, 1948.

Pearsall, Paul. *The Last Self-Help Book You'll Ever Need*. New York: Basic Books, 2005.

Peters, Tom with Waterman, Robert H. Jr. *In Search of Excellence*. London: HarperCollins Business, 1982.

Peters, Tom. *The Seminar: Crazy Times Call for Crazy Organizations*. New York: Vintage Books, 1994.

Tom, Peters. *Thriving on Chaos*. New York: Harper & Row Publishers, 1987.

Pierson, Orville. *Highly Effective Networking*. Franklin Lakes, NJ: Career Press, 2009.

Robbins, Anthony. *Unlimited Power*. London: Simon & Schuster, 1987.

Robbins, Anthony. *Awaken the Giant Within*. New York: Fireside, 1992.

Royal College of Psychiatrists. *Cognitive Behavioural Therapy (CBT)*. London: Royal College of Psychiatrists (website), 2001.

Salecl, Renata *Choice (Big Ideas)*. London: Profile, 2010.

Schiraldi, Glen R. *The Post-Traumatic Stress Disorder Sourcebook*. Los Angeles: Lowell House, 2000.

Semmelroth, Carl and Smith, Donald E.P. *The Anger Habit*. Naperville, Ill: Sourcebooks, 2000.

Silbiger, Steven. *The 10-Day MBA*. London: Judy Piatkus (Publishers), 1993.

Southon, Mike and West, Chris. *The Beermat Entrepreneur*. London: Prentice Hall Business, 2002.

Spinelli Jr. Stephen, Rosenberg, Robert M. and Birley, Sue. *Franchising*. London: Financial Times Prentice Hall, 2004.

Starr, Julie. *The Coaching Manual*. Harlow, UK: Pearson Education, 2003.

The Oxford Dictionary of Sports, Science & Medicine. Oxford, UK: Oxford University Press, 2006.

Tichy, Noel M. and Bennis, Warren G. *Judgement*, New York: Portfolio, 2007.

Timperley, John. *Network Your Way to Success*. London: Judy Piatkus (Publishers), 2002.

Tisch, Jonathan M. with Weber, Karl. *The Power of We*. Hoboken, NJ: John Wiley & Sons Inc., 2004.

Tracy, Brian. *Maximum Achievement*. New York: Fireside/Simon & Schuster, 1993.

Tracy, Brian. *Goals!* San Francisco: Berrett-Koehler, 2003.

Tracy, Brian. *Eat That Frog*. London: Hodder Mobius, 2004.

Trout, Jack. *Trout on Strategy*. New York: McGraw Hill, 2004.

Watson, Charles E. *What Smart People do When Dumb Things Happen at Work*. Franklin Lakes, NJ: Career Press, 1999.

Webb Young, James. *A Technique for Producing Ideas*. New York: McGraw Hill, 1965.

Weiner, Bernard. *Human Motivation*. Newbury Park, CA: Sage, 1992.

Wilson, Eric G. *Against Happiness*. New York: Farrar, Straus and Giroux, 2008.

Yate, Martin John. *Great Answers to Tough Interview Questions*. London: Kogan Page, 2001.

Yate, Martin John. *Hiring the Best*. Avon, MA: Adams Media Corp, 2005.

Zenger, John H., Folkman, Joseph R. and Edinger, Scott K. *The Inspiring Leader*. New York: McGraw Hill, 2009.

Zinsser, William. *On Writing Well*. New York: Harper & Row, 1976.

ABOUT ROBERT KELSEY

Robert Kelsey is a financial journalist turned City banker turned entrepreneur. Currently he is the founder and CEO of Moorgate Communications financial PR agency. He is also an author – publishing his first book, *The Pursuit of Happiness* (a "lad-lit" comedy on his life as an English banker in New York) in 2000.

Yet Robert calls himself a practitioner in failure after a childhood and early adulthood strewn with academic and career disasters. Determined to find an answer, he became a self-help addict – reading scores of books across the self-help genre.

Robert discovered that his problem wasn't failure but fear of failure. He was a classic High-FF – someone with a high fear of failure – approaching difficult but achievable challenges with a sense of dread regarding the seemingly inevitable failure that awaited him and, therefore, seeking to avoid the challenge altogether: making his inevitable failure self-fulfilling.

Yet, while helpful, the self-help books also promised something they couldn't deliver: a cure. Working with the London Association for Counselling & Psychotherapy, he discovered that, not only was his condition innate, it led him in totally the wrong direction with respect to goal-setting. Once aware of his condition, however, Robert Kelsey also realized that progress is possible as long as we take account of the fears that drive our insecurities, accept them as part of us, and find a way of navigating these self-constructed mental hurdles. *What's Stopping You?* is the result.

INDEX

Index

Index

Index

Index